THE BARRICADE AT CLICHY

Borgo Press Books by ALEXANDRE DUMAS

Anthony
The Barricade at Clichy; or, The Fall of Napoleon
Bathilda
Caligula
The Corsican Brothers (with Eugène Grangé & Xavier de Montépin)
The Count of Monte Cristo, Part One: The Betrayal of Edmond Dantès
The Count of Monte Cristo, Part Two: The Resurrection of Edmond Dantès
The Count of Monte Cristo, Part Three: The Rise of Monte Cristo
The Count of Monte Cristo, Part Four: The Revenge of Monte Cristo
A Fairy Tale (with Adolphe de Leuven and Léon Lhérie)
The Gold Thieves
Kean
The Last of the Three Musketeers; or, The Prisoner of the Bastille
    (Musketeers #3)
Lorenzino
The Mohican's War
Napoléon Bonaparte
Queen Margot
Richard Darlington (with Prosper Dinaux)
Sylvandire
The Three Musketeers (Musketeers #1)
The Three Musketeers—Twenty Years Later (Musketeers #2)
The Tower of Nesle (with Frédéric Gaillardet)
The Two Dianas (with Paul Meurice)
Urbain Grandier and the Devils of Loudon
The Venetian
The Whites and the Blues
The Widow's Husband; and, Porthos in Search of an Outfit
Young Louix XIV

RELATED DRAMAS:

The Queen's Necklace, by Pierre Decourcelle
The Seed of the Musketeers, by Paul de Kock & Guénée (Musketeers #5)
The San Felice, by Maurice Drack
The Son of Porthos the Musketeer, by Émile Blavet (Musketeers #4)
A Summer Night's Dream, Adolphe de Leuven & Joseph-Bernard Rosier
*The Widow's Husband; and, Porthos in Search of an Outfit: Two Dumasian
    Comedies*, edited by Frank J. Morlock

THE BARRICADE AT CLICHY

OR, THE FALL OF NAPOLEON
A PLAY IN FIVE ACTS

ALEXANDRE DUMAS

Translated and Adapted by Frank J. Morlock

THE BORGO PRESS
MMXII

THE BARRICADE AT CLICHY

FIRST BORGO PRESS EDITION

Published by Wildside Press LLC

www.wildsidebooks.com

DEDICATION

To Tony Smith, for many years of friendship

CONTENTS

CAST OF CHARACTERS

Emperor Napoleon

Victor

Bertrand

Fortunio

Caulaincourt, Duke of Vicenza

Emmanuel de Mérigny

The Prefect

Brisquet

Marshall Blücher

Marshall Moncey

Marshall Bertrand

Lorrain

General Michel

Bastien

Michélin

Pierre

Pointu

Bossu, the Humpback

Major of the School

Captain Campbell

A Veteran

Parliamentary Prussian

First Prussian

Second Prussian

Third Prussian

A French Member of Parliament

A Prussian Colonel

A Sapper

Cambronne

Major Koller

Jean Leroux

First Postilion

Second Postilion

Chautard

Andrieux

A Provincial

First Courier

Second Courier

Third Courier

Town Crier

Catherine

France

A Young Girl

La Calade

An Old Woman

A Servant

A Peasant

Arthur, Henry, Leon, Students of the École Polytechnique

ACT I
SCENE 1

The 26th of January 1814, a little before dawn. A square in the little town of Saint-Dizier. To the left, the house of Colonel Bertrand, behind the house a street which crosses the stage. In the back of the house, Fortune Michélin. Although it is still night, you feel the village is not sleeping. There's a light in most of the houses.

Victor and a postilion—both are on horseback and covered with mud—it's clear they've run fast at full gallop. Catherine is seated on a milestone.

VICTOR

(stopping his horse at the door of the house on the left)

Ooh!

POSTILION

I believe we've arrived, haven't we! Oh! You go at a pretty pace! Do you know how much time we took to get here?

VICTOR

(checking his watch)

An hour.

POSTILION

An hour! An hour to go three and a half leagues. Excuse me! You move like an official courier. Bad custom.

(to his horse)

Right, Blücher?

VICTOR

Say Thomas, your horse is called Blücher?

POSTILION

Yes, I call him that because he is naughty like a donkey; he only kicks—

(to horse)

Hold still a minute, will you? You see, we are measuring our grain. Give him a lot, Mr. Victor.

VICTOR

A post and a half, six francs, thirty sous; for reins, seven francs ten sous. Here, there's ten francs.

POSTILION

Is it useful to give you these fifty sous difference?

VICTOR

No, it's for Blücher.

POSTILION

Here, my good man.

VICTOR

What are you doing?

POSTILION

I'm passing your money in front of his nose.

VICTOR

Which means he would run for the King of Prussia.

POSTILION

Well, he's not called Blücher for nothing. Let's go, en route, get going.

(stopping)

By the way, Mr. Victor, you know that the Cossacks are every-where around here, right? At Toul, at Chaumont, at Bar-sur-Ornain? There's no time to lose to get your sister away, and, since I have advice to give you, (as you specifically came from Paris to find her), it's not to dawdle. Goodbye, Mr. Victor. Hop!

(He jumps back in the saddle and leaves at a trot.)

VICTOR

Thanks, my friend, thanks.

(He goes to ring the bell at the house to the left. Catherine rises and places herself between him and the door.)

CATHERINE

Mr. Victor!

VICTOR

What do you want with me, child?

CATHERINE

(raising her veil)

Don't you recognize me? You don't recognize poor Catherine, your foster sister?

VICTOR

Oh—yes indeed, my good Catherine, and what are you doing in the street at this hour?

CATHERINE

Ah! Mr. Victor, I am indeed wretched.

VICTOR

Really, I heard talk about it, my poor girl. Jean Leroux who ought to marry you, left with the last levy of 30,000 men—and was killed at Leipzig leaving you—

(hesitating)

CATHERINE

Leaving me pregnant—alas yes—hell, I'd deny it Mr. Victor. Only I cannot—everyone knows—I hid my misfortune as long as I could with old Papa Michélin but at the critical moment I had to admit it to him—he gave me fifteen days to get my strength back, then at the end of the fifteen days he put a bag of money in my hands—500 francs—all that he had in the house—then he kicked me out—me and my child.

VICTOR

And since that time, poor girl—?

CATHERINE

Since then, he won't see me again, although I spoke to him through your sister who he loves and respects as a saint now— well, even to your sister he refused.

VICTOR

Is he alone?

CATHERINE

No—he wrote to my brother Fortunio, and my brother Fortunio is with him.

VICTOR

And have you seen Fortunio?

CATHERINE

Ah—indeed, yes! He is even worse than my father. He said that if he ever found me in his path he would break my arms and legs to be certain never to meet me again.

VICTOR

Poor Catherine! And what were you doing there?

CATHERINE

Hell, Mr. Victor—it's the house I was born in—it's the house where my poor mother died—you know they say when a miser dies with a treasure buried somewhere their souls wander around the neighborhood where the treasure is buried. I am dead to the world—the treasure of my youth and my innocence is buried in that house, and my poor soul comes to wander around it—

VICTOR

And your child, Catherine?

CATHERINE

He's a boy—oh, if you could see him, beautiful like an angel, Mr. Victor! Poor little one—he doesn't know what he has cost me—Oh, he must love me a great deal to return the happiness he's stolen from me. He is a league from here—on the road to Moutier-en-Der—with my aunt Julienna.

VICTOR

Catherine, do you need anything?

CATHERINE

Thanks, Mr. Victor—I need nothing—only pity.

VICTOR

Do you want me to try to reconcile you to your brother?

CATHERINE

Try—but I have no hope—

VICTOR

No matter—you can always make the attempt. But, wait, as I have very little time for myself I will inform my sister of my arrival, and while she's dressing, I'll speak to Fortunio.

(ringing)

CATHERINE

You are really good, Victor.

VICTOR

Do you know what you must do in the meantime, Catherine?

CATHERINE

Tell me, Victor.

VICTOR

Go to the post and order two horses—have them harnessed and brought here for the carriage.

(ringing a second time)

CATHERINE

I'll run there, Victor, I'll run there.

(She leaves.)

VICTOR

Hey—you in there—are you dead?

PIERRE

(from within)

Here, here—who's ringing?

VICTOR

It's me—open up—

PIERRE

(opening a window, rifle in hand)

Who—you?

VICTOR

What? Don't you recognize me, you dog?

PIERRE

Heavens, it's our young Master. I beg your pardon. Hell, you know as the Prussians are hereabouts—we've barricaded ourselves inside.

VICTOR

Okay, okay—weren't you told of my arrival?

PIERRE

Oh, indeed. The Colonel sent us an express yesterday.

VICTOR

And where was he yesterday?

PIERRE

At Arcis-sur-Aube.

VICTOR

There—the carriage is ready?

PIERRE

Completely loaded, Mr. Victor.

VICTOR

Inform my sister of my arrival so she can dress.

PIERRE

Oh—it won't take long—because she's been expecting you at any moment. I think she wore her clothes to bed.

FRANCE

(from inside)

Brother—it's you brother.

PIERRE

There—there she is.

VICTOR

Yes, little sister, it's me.

(the door opens)

Come! Come!

FRANCE

Oh—how happy I am to see you—oh, how fearful I was—
you know the enemy is no more than four or five leagues from
here—Father wrote that you were coming to take me to Paris.
Poor daddy! He's at Arcis-sur-Aube. Did you see him on the
way?

VICTOR

No—I came by way of Chalons.

FRANCE

And the Emperor? Where is he?

VICTOR

He must have left Paris the evening of the same day I left.

FRANCE

And what are they saying at Paris? Is there any hope? The Emperor won't allow the enemy to get too close, right?

VICTOR

We must hope so, France. Meanwhile, get ready—Catherine went for the horses—you'll take Brigitte with you—tell her.

FRANCE

Oh, she won't wait—don't worry—but come on in.

VICTOR

No, I want to speak to Fortunio Michélin.

FRANCE

Ah! Yes, it's true—he's returned. You know this unfortunate Catherine—?

VICTOR

I know everything; I just saw her. Poor child! Now—there's Fortunio waking up. Let me talk with him for a minute. In ten minutes, we'll leave.

FRANCE

Hug me one more time, brother. Oh, I am so happy to see you

again.

(hugging him)

Hello, Fortunio!

FORTUNIO

(entering)

Hello, Miss France! You do me honor. Why, I'm not mistaken, it's Mr. Victor.

(hand on the police cap)

Mr. Victor!

VICTOR

Yes, it's me, my friend.

FORTUNIO

You, Mr. Victor. You left the Polytechnic Institute?

VICTOR

Yes, I got leave to come find my sister in my father's absence. But you—you've left my father?

FORTUNIO

Yes, Mr. Victor. I've returned to civilian life—I took my final dismissal. That's the way I think at the moment.

VICTOR

And how did you obtain your release?

FORTUNIO

Oh—in the simplest way. At the Review of the Emperor and King, which took place two weeks ago, I left the ranks. I pointed to my shako and I waited. He said, "Good, there's one of my veterans who has need to speak with me", and he came to me. "Ah, it's you Michélin," you know the Emperor knows me, then turning to his brother, Jerome, who was with him, "Pay no attention—it's a rifleman of honor from Marengo and a cross of honor from Wagram who needs to speak to me. Go on. What do you need?" "My discharge!" "What do you mean, your discharge?" "Yes, sir." "At the moment the enemy penetrates France, a veteran of the Pyrenees asks for his discharge? It can't be possible." "It's the way, I think, sire." "And if it's not mine?" "Oh, Your Majesty commands but he will die of shame in this case." "Who will die of shame?" "The old man who was in the Seven Years War—whose discharge was signed by Solibise— my father!" "Your father will die of shame if you don't receive your discharge—?" "Yes, sire." "Explain this to me." "He's eighty years old and he is alone." "All alone? And how did he get along until now?" "He had a daughter, my sister Catherine." "Well Catherine?" "Well, sire, she is dead."

VICTOR

What do you mean, she is dead?

FORTUNIO

Yes, Mr. Victor dead—to my way of thinking.

CATHERINE

(who has heard)

My God!

FORTUNIO

"Still, you understand, the old man is half paralyzed, he needs someone to care for him—something like a nurse; well, I leave your service for his, I get my discharge, and I become a house-wife." "Ah, you tell me too much. Your request is granted my brave fellow. Berthier this brave man has his discharge, five hundred francs pension and the cross. My compliments to the old man of the Seven Years War." "They won't fail to be delivered, Sire," and he continued on his way—I went back to the ranks, saying to myself, five hundred francs pension—two hundred fifty for the cross—total seven hundred fifty—with this one has enough bread for two or even three or four if the others were eating the bread.

VICTOR

Look—my dear Fortunio—you care for me a lot, don't you?

FORTUNIO

Do I love you! I took you from the midwife and brought you to your father, saying to him, "It's a boy, Captain, it's a boy." How you cried then—like a lamb that had lost its way. Do I love you?—not only do I love you, I respect you.

VICTOR

Well, my friend, if I were to ask you for a favor, you would do it for me?

FORTUNIO

Listen, Mr. Victor, I see you come zigzagging—let's not get embroidered in cross purposes and speak frankly—you are getting at Catherine right?

VICTOR

My dear Fortunio.

FORTUNIO

You do me honor—but here is what is agreed in the Army—illegitimate children, born outside of marriage were only received as ornaments on a Russian, Austrian or Prussian flag—no matter which. It was the duty of the father or the mother to obtain the paper which straightened things out—the baptism of fire legitimizing the child. That was our way of thinking.

VICTOR

So!

FORTUNIO

So—let them wrap the kid in paper of the type I've mentioned and bring him to me, and if he had a tail as long as the Emperor of Austria's—which is unlikely—I would say "That's my nephew." Until then, I don't know who Catherine is.

(he looks to his side)

But she'd better not chance reappearing in front of my eyes, nor those of my father—that's advice I would give her—bon voyage, Mr. Victor—and the best compliments to the colonel.

VICTOR

And you're staying here with your father? Aren't you fearful?

FORTUNIO

What should I be afraid of, Mr. Victor?

VICTOR

That the Prussians, the Austrians, or the Cossacks won't recognize you for a pensioner and take you prisoner.

FORTUNIO

Me? What for since I lost the clarinet and sold the cabbage cutter—anyway, I don't worry about the Prussians, the Austrians or the Cossacks.

VICTOR

It seem to me you've found yourself face to face with them more than once.

FORTUNIO

Ah, yes—in foreign lands, but not at home. Listen carefully to this. So long as the Little Corporal is alive, they won't dare cross the frontier and in Lorrain and Champagne you know— Prussians don't grow.

VICTOR

But if you're told they are six leagues from here?

FORTUNIO

It's not true!

VICTOR

If they tell you their avant garde is at the Bar-sur-Ornain and at Bar-sur-Seine? If they tell you the Old Guard met them yesterday at Columbey-les-Deux-Églises and that there was an engagement?

FORTUNIO

And the result of the engagement?

VICTOR

The old guard is retreating to Troyes.

(Enter some peasants who are fleeing.)

FORTUNIO

It's not true!

VICTOR

Why, who do you take all these poor people for? Look!

FORTUNIO

For poltroons, at least, that's my way of thinking.

(he goes back in.)

CATHERINE

Thanks, Mr. Victor!

VICTOR

You heard?

CATHERINE

Yes, where is the French army?

VICTOR

Two or three leagues from here—on the route to Châlons and Arcis-sur-Aube.

CATHERINE

That's far.

VICTOR

Where are you going?

CATHERINE

Your father is there, Mr. Victor. I am going to beg him to accept me in his regiment as a vivandiere and the first flag taken from the enemy—if a good chap takes it—he will give me a part of it.

VICTOR

Go child and commend yourself to me.

CATHERINE

You are really good, Mr. Victor. Goodbye.

CATHERINE

Goodbye, Catherine.

(Exit Catherine.)

VICTOR

Come on, France! Come on, Brigitte.

FRANCE

Here I am, brother.

VICTOR

(to postilion)

Well, what news, Bernard?

BERNARD

Bad, sir, bad.

FRANCE

You don't know if Emmanuel has returned, my friend?

BERNARD

No, miss.

VICTOR

What Emmanuel? Emmanuel de Mégrigny—our cousin. Could some accident have happened to him?

FRANCE

I'm afraid it may. Day before yesterday, his mother received a letter that he was leaving for Troyes—and she had not seen him yet.

BERNARD

Ah, damn—if he encountered Cossacks!

FRANCE

Well—?

BERNARD

Wait! Here are poor people who've been plundered by them two leagues from here—the man even received a lance wound in his arm.

VICTOR

The wretches! Come, sister.

FRANCE

But brother—perhaps they are in need—perhaps they have no money—let—

VICTOR

(distributing money to the fugitives)

Here my friends, here—

FUGITIVES

Thanks, young gentleman, thanks, beautiful lady.

(People surround them and others shout.)

VICTOR

What's going on?

BERNARD

Shall I bring the carriage forward?

VICTOR

No need—we are going there. Take care of yourself, Fortunio.

FORTUNIO

(arranging an armchair before the door)

Don't worry, in a little corner there's a musket near the old man from when he was a musketeer in the Forest of Der.

VICTOR

(leaving)

Goodbye.

FORTUNIO

Goodbye, Mr. Victor and everybody.

PEASANT

God protect you, my pretty Miss. God protect you—brave young man!

(The whole town is an uproar after Victor and France leave. People come and go, questioning those who pass by. They sense the approach the enemy.)

A MAN

(questioning the fugitives)

And the Cossacks—where did they meet you?

PEASANT

Between Chamouilett and Ancerville.

A WOMAN

There they plundered you?

PEASANT

As you see—robbed and beaten.

BRISQUET

Is it true that some of them carry bows and arrows?

A WOMAN

Yes, and lances two feet long with hooks at the end.

BRISQUET

Why, they're really savages then? Say—if I climb up on a roof,
I can tell you where they are.

ALL

Right—right.

(Brisquet climbs on a roof.)

FORTUNIO

(escorting Michélin to the armchair he has prepared for him)

Here, father—install yourself here—the place isn't warm but
it's a lot better in comparison to those that kissed our ears in
Moscow.

Michélin

Why's everybody here, Fortunio?

FORTUNIO

Nothing! Nothing!

Michélin

What are they saying?

FORTUNIO

Stupid things.

Michélin

Why are they running about like that?

FORTUNIO

Today's Sunday and they are having a good time.

PIERRE

Are you up there, Brisquet?

BRISQUET

(on the roof)

Yes, I'm here.

PIERRE

Well—what do you see?

BRISQUET

Oh—the field—it's completely black.

A WOMAN

Are they coming this way?

BRISQUET

Yes—some are coming by way of Moutier-en-Der—and then others still by way of Vitry-le-Français.

(The alarm bell sounds.)

PIERRE

Right! And the alarm—where's that coming from?

BRISQUET

Oh! It's Chancenay burning.

PIERRE

Ah—why if they're plundering the poor people, if they're burning villages, they must still be revenging themselves a little.

BRISQUET

Oh—down there—down there, there on the road to Betancourt—oh, they are on horseback—they're coming this way—not sparing the horses—they are entering the town. The Cossacks! The Cossacks!

(Shouts can be heard. 'The Cossacks! The Cossacks!' Alarm. Everyone flees the doors and the windows are shut. The Tocsins continue to ring.)

FORTUNIO

Ah, decidedly it's them. This time, it would be better to take father inside—he's fragile at this age. Come, come, father—go in, go back in.

ALL

(fleeing)

The Cossacks! The Cossacks!

(The Cossacks passing through at a gallop.)

Hurrah—hurrah! Hurrah!

(Fortunio closes the door in front of him. A last Cossack passes by and seeing a door shutting draws a pistol from his belt and fires into the door. A cry can be heard.)

COSSACK

Hurrah!

(passing through)

(He disappears with his companions. The door reopens.)

(Enter Michélin, wounded in the neck and dying in Fortunio's arms. Fortunio lets Michélin slide from his arms to the ground.

FORTUNIO

Oh, the scoundrels! Oh, the bastards! Father—say something, father.

Michélin

Huh! Huh!

FORTUNIO

Yes, I understand what you mean. "Vengeance!" Don't worry, father, you will be avenged.

(People come out of their houses.)

A MAN

There was a musket shot fired.

PIERRE

No, it was from a pistol.

(they notice the group of Fortunio and his father)

Oh—look at the old man—he's covered with blood.

ANOTHER MAN

What's the matter, Fortunio? What's wrong?

FORTUNIO

Some brigands killed an old man of eighty—as if it were worth the trouble to kill a man of that age when they are busy dying by themselves.

MAN

Killed? Killed? Oh, no, no, a doctor—a surgeon.

FORTUNIO

Oh—no use. I've seen some like this in my life and I know

he's finished. Goodbye, old man! You know what I said. Don't worry. Here, my friends, help me to put him on his bed.

PIERRE

That's all we need—to murder folks. Doesn't that enrage you? Doesn't it make you want to run these swine back to their Caucasus?

MAN

But why are you shutting yourself in?

FORTUNIO

(somberly)

It's my way of thinking.

BRISQUET

(on the roof)

Oh—there's yet another village burning down there—it's Villiers.

(the clock rings)

Alarm! Alarm! Here's the enemy. The Prussians.

ALL

To arms!

(The horns of the approaching Prussians can be heard. A regiment enters the town. At the moment when the Colonel appears in the center of the town, a window opens in Michélin's house. Fortunio appears with his musket, aims at the Colonel and fires. The colonel falls.)

FORTUNIO

Neck for neck—

(Cries—tumult. The Prussians break ranks. Some try to break downs the doors of the house—others set it on fire.)

MAJOR

Two houses for the solders to pillage. Then set fire to the town. Go to it!

(Fortunio reappears at his window, aims and fires at the Major. The Major falls.)

FORTUNIO

I win the prize! That's my way of thinking.

(He escapes to the roof and slides down the other side in the midst of numerous shots not one of which strikes him. The sound of French drums beating out the charge come from the other side.)

BRISQUET

(on the room)

Oh! The French! The French! Long live the French!

(At shouts of the French, the French some doors and windows reopen and shots are fired from the openings. The charges comes closer. The Cossacks reappear and run off in disorder.)

(The Prussians beat the retreat. The French appear. There is a fusillade. Colonel Bertrand at the head of his regiment takes the square, house by house. The Emperor appears.)

VOICES

The Emperor! The Emperor! Long live the Emperor.

BRISQUET

(waving the Tricolor)

Long live the Emperor.

(All the inhabitants leave their houses shouting 'Long live the Emperor!)

EMPEROR

I am here, children—do not fear. Colonel Bertrand, pursue the Prussians until you meet serious resistance, and then come back and find me if possible with one or two prisoners.

BERTRAND

(pointing to his house)

Sire, there's my house—it's at the disposition of Your Majesty—Pierre open up everything—light everything up—

EMPEROR

Thanks, Colonel. Perhaps I'll do that. While waiting, I have to talk with these brave people. I want them to see me, I want them to touch me, I want them to feel me in their midst.

ALL

Long live the Emperor!

EMPEROR

A table and a chair—that's all I ask.

BERTRAND

A table and a chair for the Emperor.

(to Pierre)

And my son and daughter, Pierre?

PIERRE

Left an hour ago for Paris, Colonel.

BERTRAND

That's wonderful—

(soldiers)

Forward, friends, forward!

(The people rush into the square.)

A MAN

Oh, sire, sire! Here you are! What joy! We have nothing to fear now, the Emperor is with us.

EMPEROR

Thanks, my friends, thanks! Well, let's see—what's going on?

PIERRE

Sire, everything around here is on fire—we are surrounded by enemies and they were here just now—all rogues, the brigands, and they killed a man.

EMPEROR

A man from the village?

PIERRE

Yes, sire—an old man of eighty.

EMPEROR

The wretches! Bertrand!

BERTRAND

Sire?

EMPEROR

Fire hundred francs for the family.

FORTUNIO

(reappearing with his musket)

No need, Sire.

EMPEROR

Ah, it's you, Michélin! Why no need?

PIERRE

Because he was my father.

EMPEROR

Your father, my poor Michélin?

FORTUNIO

Yes—the old man—the old man from the Seven Years War.

EMPEROR

Wasn't it to care for him that you requested your discharge?

FORTUNIO

Yes, Sire—but the poor old fellow no longer needs anything—
except—

EMPEROR

To be avenged, right?

FORTUNIO

Oh! As to that, he ought to be satisfied. I hit both the Colonel
and the Major of the regiment that my Colonel is pursuing.
That's not what would please him.

EMPEROR

Well—what would?—speak.

FORTUNIO

Well, what would please him is that when they bury him, the drums beat him a little march—bam—bam—with a rifle salute—which would remind him of his wars—he always wanted that, poor old chap, at his funeral. That was his way of thinking.

EMPEROR

Fine. It will be done.

FORTUNIO

Thanks, my Emperor.

EMPEROR

Let's see—child—which of you can give me intelligence?

EMMANUEL

(coming forward)

I, Sire, if your Majesty will allow.

EMPEROR

You—so be it—come here.

(sitting near the table)

What do you know?

EMMANUEL

I can tell Your Majesty precisely where the enemy is.

EMPEROR

Where the enemy is?

EMMANUEL

In returning from Bar-sur-Aube I was taken by the Prussians and escorted to Blücher who kept me for two days. I only escaped a quarter of an hour ago.

EMPEROR

How was that?

EMMANUEL

A French regiment, guided by a young girl from this village—the sister of a soldier who just now had the honor of speaking to Your Majesty—fell suddenly on the Prussian encampment so that in the midst of the disorder, I was able to escape by jumping on a horse and I came to reassure my mother who thought I was lost.

EMPEROR

And what can you tell me?

EMMANUEL

Sire, Marshall Blücher and General Lanskoi spent the night

at Bar-sur-Aube and must be, at the moment near Brienne, marching towards Troyes to help the Austrians. The Corps we just met here is that of General Lanskoi, who follows General Sachem. The troops remaining in the rear are those of General York, ordered to contain the garrison of Metz.

EMPEROR

Ah! Ah! So we've just cut Blücher's army in two, at the moment, when it crossed from Lorraine to Champagne.

EMMANUEL

Exactly, Sire.

EMPEROR

How do you know all this, Sir?

EMMANUEL

They were unaware I knew German so they didn't hide things from me.

EMPEROR

Who are you, Sir?

EMMANUEL

Sire, I am Emmanuel de Mérigny, the nephew of Colonel Bertrand.

EMPEROR

Good—what do you do?

EMMANUEL

I am studying surgery at Troyes—I was coming to see my mother, whom I didn't wish to leave alone and exposed in the midst of enemies when I was captured by the Prussians.

EMPEROR

Would you like to be attached to my staff?

EMMANUEL

Sire, that would be such a great honor that I dare not hope it.

EMPEROR

That's fine. Bertrand—inscribe this young man.

BERTRAND

(returning)

Sire.

EMPEROR

Well, Colonel—?

BERTRAND

Sire, I don't think we have strong forces facing us. I had the regiment halt a quarter of a league from the town where it will remain on watch until the time Your Majesty recalls it.

EMPEROR

Fine, my dear Colonel.

BERTRAND

Your Majesty has positive intelligence?

EMPEROR

Yes—and it comes from someone you know—come forward Mr. de Mérigny.

BERTRAND

Emmanuel.

EMMANUEL

My dear Uncle.

EMPEROR

Look—embrace each other.

BERTRAND

Your Majesty doesn't deign to enter my house.

EMPEROR

Thanks—we are leaving in ten minutes. We must save Troyes, we will leave a rear guard here—we will cross the Forest of Der with good guides. At Brienne we will return to the hunt. Gentlemen—you hear—we're crossing the Forest of Der—let orders be given accordingly—

(rolls of drums)

What's that?

BERTRAND

Sire, it's the honor guard of poor Michélin—an old soldier.

(Michélin's body in its uniform of the Seven Years War, hat and saber at his feet—the drums beat. The soldiers reverse arms.)

CATHERINE

(running a flag in her hand)

Here brother, to make the little one's swaddling clothes.

FORTUNIO

You are mistaken, Catherine, it's to make a shroud for Father.

(He throws the flag on the corpse; the guard passes. The Emperor removes his hat.)

CURTAIN

ACT I
SCENE 2

The Grenaux farm. A room where the walls are crenellated.

BASTIEN

Come, come, lads, there's no use getting killed for nothing. It's the entire Prussian army—it's too big a mouthful for us to swallow. Hide in the cellar, put the muskets in the hiding place, leave by the exit and each go to his work—some to the plow, others to sowing, others to the barn. And if these scoundrels give us trouble well, we'll see.

BRISQUET

But you, Papa Bastien.

BASTIEN

Oh, don't worry about me. I'll wait for them. I'm master of the house. I have to do the honors for them. Go—but hurry up.

BRISQUET

The Prussians know me. I saw them at Saint Dizier. I prefer not to see them again. They are very ugly.

BASTIEN

Good. Everything is ready.

(he stretches out on two boxes of straw and pretends to sleep)

BRISQUET

And me, and me, Papa Bastien?

BASTIEN

Will you let me sleep, Brisquet?

(he snores)

(The Prussians and Blücher appear at the door—bayonets extended.)

BRISQUET

Oh, Messieurs les Prussians don't hurt me.

BLÜCHER

Is there someone here?

BRISQUET

Papa Bastien is here—see—there sleeping.

BLÜCHER

Wake him.

A SOLDIER

(helping Bastien)

He doesn't want to wake up. I'm going to tickle him with the point of my bayonet.

BASTIEN

(who has been struck in the rear)

Huh?

BLÜCHER

It seems we've finally found someone who can speak. What's become of these devilish peasants? They must have gone to earth like foxes—answer to Marshal Blücher!

BASTIEN

To Marshal Blücher?

BRISQUET

(aside)

What? That's the name of Thomas' horse—the one that's naughty like a donkey—

BASTIEN

Indeed, the honor—

BLÜCHER

We don't want to do you any harm—we only want some information.

BASTIEN

Some information? Indeed, an honor, general. I am ready to
give it to you.

BLÜCHER

Where are we! What's the name of this farm?

BASTIEN

Here?

BLÜCHER

Yes, here.

BASTIEN

Come on—you are kidding me. You know quite well where you
are.

BLÜCHER

If I knew, I wouldn't be asking you, imbecile!

BASTIEN

Such an honor, general—well, you are at Montmirail, eh! And
this farm is called The Farm of Grenaux, you see—why because
the owner of this farm is named Pace.

BLÜCHER

What's the relation between Mr. Pace and the name of this Grenaux Farm?

BASTIEN

Because it's his.

BLÜCHER

There's nothing to be got from this clown.

BASTIEN

So honored, general—

BLÜCHER

Look—have you got any food to eat on your farm?

BASTIEN

Ah—yes, damn—there's leg of lamb on the spit which is 3 days old.

BRISQUET

It must be rotten.

BLÜCHER

What do you mean, three days old?

BASTIEN

Ah, yes—because for three days they've been saying the Prussians are coming, the Prussians are coming—So, I said, well, if the Prussians are coming we'd better prepare food for them—and as I had leg of lamb, I prepared leg of lamb for you.

BRISQUET

(aside)

What an ass-kisser—

BASTIEN

Don't you want some?

BLÜCHER

Indeed! So bring your leg of lamb.

BASTIEN

Such an honor, general.

BRISQUET

(aside)

It will be peppery—that one.

(Bastien goes out.)

BLÜCHER

All the same, gentleman, you know it's only a rest w'ere taking here—it's a question of being first in Paris—they say General York is at Château Thierry—that General Sachem is at la Ferte—we are late.

BASTIEN

(returning)

Eh! No—you're not late for dinner—it's only two o'clock.

BLÜCHER

We're not late for dinner—we're late getting to Paris.

BASTIEN

To Paris—? You are going to Paris?

BLÜCHER

Certainly.

BASTIEN

In that case, I'll go, too.

BLÜCHER

How many leagues from here to Paris?

BASTIEN

You do me honor, general, twenty-three.

BLÜCHER

Say friend—the farm is fortified.

(to Bastien, pointing to the loopholes)

What's all this?

BASTIEN

Saving your respect, General, it's a hole.

BLÜCHER

Yes, but who made that loophole?

BASTIEN

The French, General.

BRISQUET

Stool pigeon, go!

BASTIEN

They passed, and they said, "Here's a fine position, necessary to defend." Then they made their loopholes, but I told them you will ruin the walls. They chased me off.

BLÜCHER

Well, what did you say to them, then?

BASTIEN

I said, "You do me great honor," and I went away.

BLÜCHER

Decidedly this man is an idiot—to dinner, gentleman, to dinner.

BRISQUET

(low to Bastien)

Look, why did you tell him—?

BASTIEN

Leave off, I'm confusing them.

BRISQUET

What?

(Bastien whispers in his ear)

Ah, good! Choke Thomas' horse!

AIDE DE CAMP

(entering)

The Field Marshal?

BLÜCHER

Come in, sir—well what news of that cannonade yesterday?

AIDE DE CAMP

Milord, it seems there was a hard fight.

BLÜCHER

Where?

AIDE DE CAMP

Near Champaubert.

BLÜCHER

With some separated French column.

AIDE DE CAMP

No, your Excellency—with a corps of the whole army.

BLÜCHER

Commanded by Raguse, Trévise, Tarente?

AIDE DE CAMP

No Excellency—commanded by Napoleon in person.

BLÜCHER

By Napoleon? He is at Brienne, sir.

AIDE DE CAMP

I fear Your Excellency may be mistaken. It appears that the Emperor arrived yesterday by the route from Nogent to Sézanne.

BLÜCHER

I had that road checked, it is impracticable.

AIDE DE CAMP

Not for him, Milord.

BLÜCHER

Well—he met general Alsufief?

AIDE DE CAMP

Yes, Milord, and it appears that he defeated him.

BLÜCHER

What the devil are you saying, sir?

AIDE DE CAMP

That's what we've just learned from the deserters.

BLÜCHER

(rising)

Deserters? And Alsufief—what happened to him?

AIDE DE CAMP

He was taken, Milord.

BLÜCHER

What do you mean, taken?

AIDE DE CAMP

With the two generals under his orders, a fifth of the officers, and eighteen hundred men.

AN OFFICER

The French are appearing from the route of Champaubert.

AIDE DE CAMP

What did I have the honor to tell Your Excellency?

BLÜCHER

What? They have the audacity to attack us—? What's that? The forward posts are meeting them? To arms, gentlemen, to arms.

(The charge is sounded; the battle begins—the Prussians fire from inside the house—bullets pierce the walls—the wounded fall, the dying also—suddenly musket shots pass through the floor. The Prussians are attacked from within and without—the farm collapses.)

BLACKOUT

ACT I
SCENE 3

The battle continues on all sides. The distance is hidden in smoke. The sun sets. The French seize possession of the battle-field over which the moon rises. The Emperor appears. He is received in the midst of the ruins of the farm by the peasants.

EMPEROR

It's okay, my friends, it's okay—you are brave hearts—brave Frenchmen; and you, and the earth of France devour them to the last man—Berthier.

BERTHIER

Sir?

EMPEROR

Send a man instantly to Chatillon to inform Caulaincourt that yesterday I defeated the Prussians at Champaubert and today I defeated the Prussians at Montmirail and that in three days I will defeat the Austrians at Montereau—take up the dead, gentleman—I will sleep here.

ALL

Long live the Emperor!

CURTAIN

ACT II
SCENE 4

The 26th and 27th of February, a bivouac in the vicinity of Méry-au-Bar. Night. The Emperor's tent is visible, a lamp is on the post. The iron bed is under the tent.

BERTRAND

You say the Emperor went to make a reconnaissance?

OFFICER

Yes, Colonel—near Pont-sur-Seine.

BERTRAND

This is where we are camping, gang—

FORTUNIO

Well, there's one good thing. Tonight we won't have water up to our ankles.

LORRAIN

Are you're shoes full of water?

FORTUNIO

Yes, to the collar of my jacket. Let's recapitulate—in Egypt, roasted, in Russia, frozen, in France; drowned. It would be hard to say which of these three deaths is the most agreeable. Give a drink to the brat, Catherine.

CATHERINE

He's not thirsty.

FORTUNIO

(drinking from the canteen)

They're always thirsty. A drop to the kid.

CATHERINE

No, no—it will make him sick.

FORTUNIO

Eau de vie—? Never.

(to child)

Drink, uncle.

CHILD

(weeping)

Okay.

CATHERINE

Don't do him any harm, okay!

LORRAIN

Oh, right. But I thought you wanted to throw this citizen into the Marne.

FORTUNIO

It's true, but that was before he was baptized in the name— Napoleon Michélin and he hadn't been recognized by the regiment, legitimized, decorated by His Majesty, the Emperor with the yellow and black sash—now it's another matter.

LORRAIN

Heavens, it's true; what is it?

FORTUNIO

The sash from an Austrian flag that his mother took in the battle of Moutier-en- Der—where she first took arms. That this necktie was put around his neck by the Emperor's own hands—and in turn she decorated the kid. That's better than the cordon blue put on a prince when he is born—or so it seems to me. That's my way of thinking.

BERTRAND

The Emperor, gentlemen, the Emperor!

(The Emperor rides in on horseback with three or four superior officers also mounted.)

EMPEROR

Any news of the battle we heard all day near Méry-sur-Seine?

BERTRAND

The first ordinance officer went to get intelligence, sire.

GENERAL MICHEL

(in the wings)

Where is the Emperor? Where is the Emperor?

EMPEROR

This way, sir, this way!

(General Michel enters.)

EMPEROR

Ah—it's you, Michel?

(to soldiers)

Stand aside—well—what is it?

GENERAL MICHEL

Great news, Sire.

EMPEROR

Good or bad, sir?

GENERAL MICHEL

The Emperor shall judge—it's not simply a detachment of the Austrian army that General Boyer and his guard just met at Méry—as Your Majesty thought—it's the whole army.

EMPEROR

Whose?

GENERAL MICHEL

That of Blücher.

EMPEROR

You are mistaken, sir, the army of Blücher no longer exists. I destroyed it at Champaubert, at Montmirail, at Château-Thierry, and at Vauchamps. You are sure of what you say, sir?

GENERAL MICHEL

I got this information from prisoners taken today by General Boyer, sire—the Cossacks are flooding the plain and I had great trouble escaping them. I think that Your Majesty is poorly protected on the side of the Seine.

EMPEROR

Do you think these wretches would have the audacity to attack me almost in my camp? You do them too much honor, sir— these are birds of prey of the crow and vulture species. They only fight with the dead. But let's get back to Blücher—you say—

GENERAL MICHEL

I said, Sire, that he camped on the 23rd at the junction of the Aube and the Seine with 50,000 men, that there he still received reinforcements of 9,000 men, from a corps belonging to General Langeon, so it's 60,000 men that Your Majesty faces and not thirty or forty thousand.

EMPEROR

And you think that Blücher was at the Méry-sur-Seine in person?

GENERAL MICHEL

He was indeed there, Sire—he was wounded in the leg and—

(A lot of noise is heard—several shots from muskets and pistols—then shouts—the Cossacks!)

EMPEROR

(rushing quickly from his tent. At the same moment, the theatre is invaded by a swarm of Cossacks)

The Cossacks!

(The Emperor is surrounded and disappears in the midst of the horses. A Cossack goes to pierce him with his lance when Bertrand kills the Cossack with a sword blow. Struggle and confusion for a moment. Bertrand receives a lance thrust in the breast. Soldiers and Generals fire. The Cossacks are driven off but there is a moment of stupor among all the men when they realize the marauders have had the audacity to penetrate into the midst of the French camp even to the Emperor's tent.)

EMPEROR

(to General Michel)

That's well, sir. Go get two hours sleep and be ready to leave for Paris in two hours.

(to Bertrand)

Thanks, Bertrand, thanks my brave colonel. Without you, I think the war would have been over. Tell me what you want, Bertrand, and if it is in my power to fulfill your desire, your request is granted in advance—in the name of my wife and my son.

BERTRAND

(choking)

Sire—

EMPEROR

Eh, what's wrong with you?

BERTRAND

I think I am wounded, Sire.

EMPEROR

A surgeon, gentlemen, a surgeon. Colonel Bertrand is wounded.

EMMANUEL

(rushing up)

You are wounded, Colonel?

EMPEROR

In my tent, Mr. de Mérigny! Gentlemen, I think there's no need to tell you to keep a careful guard—you've just seen that's not an exaggerated precaution. You know I am expecting the Duke of Vicenza who should arrive tonight from Châtillon. Bring him. As to the rest, let all bearers of intelligence come to me.

(returning under his tent to Emmanuel)

Well, sir?

EMMANUEL

Happily, Sire, the lance struck a medallion the colonel was wearing on his breast—the medallion which contained pictures of his wife and children is broken, but it turned the lance aside so it only penetrated the skin—the wound presents no danger, Sire.

EMPEROR

No matter. Bertrand, you will sleep near me in my tent—they'll place a mattress on the ground for you—you will still be better than on bivouac.

(The soldiers form bundles into a mattress. They prepare a bed for Bertrand.)

AN OFFICER

Sire, the Duke of Vicenza has just passed the outposts.

EMPEROR

Let him come, let him come! I am waiting for him.

OFFICER

He's following me, Sire.

EMPEROR

Ah, come, come Caulaincourt, you've come from Châtillon?

DUKE

Yes, Sire.

EMPEROR

Well, I hope my victories at Chambanbert, Montmirail, Château and Vauchamps have somewhat diminished the demands of the Allies and that they grant me the left bank of the Rhine and Italy.

DUKE

Sire, indeed, this glorious week which brought us the victory bulletins in six days has echoed even to Châtillon.

EMPEROR

Then you bring me better conditions, my dear Duke.

DUKE

Sire, if there were only Russia—

EMPEROR

Well?

DUKE

But there's England, Prussia, and Austria.

EMPEROR

(impatiently)

Well.

DUKE

England will never cede Anvers to you—Prussia will never cede Coblentz to you—Austria will never cede Milan to you.

EMPEROR

(still more impatiently)

Well?

DUKE

Well, Sire, the allied sovereigns deny any designs on Frankfurt, and if Your Majesty wishes peace....

EMPEROR

Certainly, Sir, I wish it, I will say more—I shall have it.

DUKE

Sire, they demand that France return to its ancient borders.

EMPEROR

To its ancient borders! And it's you Caulaincourt, you whose heart is so essentially French—come to me with such proposals?

DUKE

Sire, it's precisely because I am French at heart that I not only bring these proposals to Your Majesty but I recommend them to you.

EMPEROR

Why have you gone crazy? What! You urge me to sign such a treaty? Have you forgotten the oath I took when taking the crown—"I swear to maintain the integrity of the territory of the Republic and to govern only with a view to the happiness and glory of the French people?"

DUKE

Sire, the happiness of a people comes before its glory—the French people thanks to Your Majesty are the most glorious of people—give them peace, Sire, and you will have given them everything.

EMPEROR

But, Duke, you forget my resources. France was less powerful, less strong, less rich, less populous in 1792 when levees en masse delivered the County in the year seven; when the battle of Zurich stopped the invasion by all Europe in the year eight;

when the battle of Marengo saved the country.

DUKE

Yes, Sire, it's true—but then she possessed what she has since lost—enthusiasm. In those days she fought for liberty.

EMPEROR

And what is she fighting for today, sir? And what am I, if not European liberty? When I took France, totally feverish from her revolution, France was to ideas and to deeds, so far in advance of other peoples that she had disturbed the European equilibrium. An Alexander was needed to tame this Bucephalous, an Androcles for this lion—what did I do? I selected what was most noble, most brave, most intelligent in France and I spread it throughout Europe. Everywhere I've gone, I have disseminated liberty into the world, like a sower of wheat. Let them wait a year, two years, ten, and they will see it grow fully developed in each furrow excavated by my cannon balls. That the Allied Sovereigns wish to see my fall, I understand, for I've proclaimed the most holy dogma ever uttered by a human mouth. I have proclaimed equality.

DUKE

Sire, it seems to me that before Your Majesty, the Convention—

EMPEROR

Yes, sir, but do you understand the difference that exists between us? The Convention proclaimed an equality which debased and I proclaimed an equality which ennobled. Do you know why its work will be treated with skepticism by posterity in the centuries to come, while mine will be blessed, although we both participated in the work. It's because they lowered the great to the foot of the scaffold where I raised the small to the foot of the throne. Go, go, sir, I am still stronger than they think. They take me quite simply for a man, for a king, for an emperor. I am more than that, sir, I am a nation.

DUKE

Sire, France believes you've done everything for your ambition and nothing for France.

EMPEROR

The truth is like the sun: Winter can obscure it, hide it even— but prosperity has its Spring—and a day will come this Spring will be eternal. I bequeath my body to the tomb, my soul to God, and my memory to posterity. Anyway, sir—I have a sure way to prevent posterity of accusing me of egotism and that is if France falls, to fall with her—if France dies, not to survive her.

DUKE

Sire, those who wish to die are not always killed—you've seen that clearly at Montereau and at Arcis-sur-Aube.

EMPEROR

One isn't always sure of being killed, it is true—but one is always sure of dying—you cannot always find a cannon ball like Turenne or like Berwick—but you can always find a pistol like Beaurepaire.

DUKE

Then, Your Majesty refuses the conditions of the Allied Sovereigns?

EMPEROR

I refuse them. Return to them, sir—tell them that the unheard of reversals have torn from me the promise to renounce the conquests I have made. But to abandon those made by others before me,—I treasure the heritage that has been placed under the care of my honor, at the price of so much effort in blood and victories. Can I leave France less than I found her? God preserve me from such shame! I reject the treaty; it is a bad treaty you offer me, Duke.

DUKE

Peace is always good, Sire—if it is quick enough.

EMPEROR

It will always be too quick if it is shameful. Go, sir, get a little rest, and return.

DUKE

Before going, shall I come for the Emperor's orders?

EMPEROR

If I want to see you—I will have you told. Go.

(Exit the Duke.)

EMPEROR

Mr. de Mérigny?

EMMANUEL

(coming forward)

Sire?

EMPEROR

(on his camp bed)

Are you a good chemist, sir?

EMMANUEL

Sire, it's the science on which I pride myself the most.

EMPEROR

Sir, swear to me on your honor, to faithfully execute the orders I am going to give you.

EMMANUEL

On my honor, I swear it.

EMPEROR

You saw what happened just now. Without your uncle, I would have been taken prisoner. You heard what Caulaincourt said. In the struggle I am undertaking, I may be overcome. I wish to be in every case and at all times—sure of my death. Napoleon must not survive Napoleon. The Emperor must not be a trophy in the hands of the Cossacks. Prepare a sure poison for me—a last friend on whom I can count, who will replace for me the slave of the Romans who held the sword on which a defeated general fell.

EMMANUEL

Oh! Sire! What are you exacting from me?

EMPEROR

The same service that Hannibal exacted from his doctor before the battle of Zama. Like Hannibal, I've crossed the Alps—Like Hannibal I've fought battles at Trébia, Cannes and Trasiméne— like Hannibal I can be betrayed by the Senate. Like Hannibal, I can wear death on my finger.

EMMANUEL

Sire, couldn't you charge someone else with this terrible honor?

EMPEROR

No—for you are young, sir, and consequently incapable of treason.

EMMANUEL

Oh—my God! What must I do?

BERTRAND

(from his bed)

Obey, Emmanuel.

EMMANUEL

Sire, I am at your orders.

EMPEROR

Here are two rings, sir—that I have made for this purpose. You see my resolve was not taken today. How long will it take you to finish your work?

EMMANUEL

Sire, in less than ten minutes.

EMPEROR

Go to the ambulance and take what you need from the pharmacy. I will wait for you.

EMMANUEL

Will Your Majesty formally repeat the order he's given me?

EMPEROR

Formally, sir, go.

(Exit Emmanuel.)

EMPEROR

(to ordinance officer)

No one came during my conversation with the Duke of Vicenza?

AN OFFICER

Three couriers have arrived, Sire, and here are their dispatches.

EMPEROR

(tearing open the first)

From Italy. What! Eugene cannot send me the 20,000 men I've asked him for! Murat has declared against me!

(opening the second)

D'Augerau—he's crossed the Saone and gone to Vesoul—he writes from there—

AN OFFICER

Read, Sire.

EMPEROR

What! He's amusing himself fighting with Bubna—to shut him up in Geneva—he has his Quarters—General at Lons-le-Saulnier—it's from Lons-le-Saulnier that he writes me—but he's going to open up the passage of the Saone.

AN OFFICER

Alas, Sire, it's already happened.

EMPEROR

Oh—the wretch. He's missed the chance to save France! Marshall Suchet will leave this instant to take command of Lyon. Bertheir will send him my orders—

(opening the third)

Trevise! From Château-Thierry—and why not from Soissons?

AN OFFICER

Crossing the valley of the Aisne, he found Soissons had been taken.

EMPEROR

Soissons taken! Rusca let Soissons be taken from me?

AN OFFICER

Sire, the first cannon ball fired by the enemy cut him in two.

EMPEROR

Oh, truly, this is worse than misfortune—this is fate. Wherever I am—victory. Wherever I am not—defeat. I need the three heads of Geryon and the hundred arms of Briarée from Brienne to Troyes—from Troyes to Champaubert—from Champaubert to Montmirail—from Montmirail to Château-Thierry—from Vauchamps to Montereau—why, I shall tire myself with all these tiger like leaps—gentlemen—give orders to get as many troops around me as possible—let all the men come from Sézanne to Villeneuve and Marigny. Tomorrow I must deal with Blücher—leave me gentlemen, leave me—I need to be alone.

(All retire except Bertrand.)

EMPEROR

Yes—leave me alone. Human power has its limits. One day strength will abandon me. This time, it will be betrayal of nature—the last—the most terrible betrayal. Oh—that Arab proverb "Better to be seated than standing, better to be lying down than seated, better to be dead than lying down."

(lying on his couch)

The fact is there must be peace in the tomb. There's peace there and peace is so good.

EMMANUEL

(entering)

Sire!

EMPEROR

Ah! I didn't think I was such a powerful enchanter! I invoked death and here it is.

EMMANUEL

Sire—here is what Your Majesty asked of me.

EMPEROR

What kind of poison is it?

EMMANUEL

A concentration of opium.

EMPEROR

And how long will it take to kill me?

EMMANUEL

Five minutes.

EMPEROR

That's long! Sir, you are a surgeon-major.

EMMANUEL

Thanks, Sire—but I confess to Your Majesty I would prefer to owe my rank to a less sad service.

EMPEROR

You're wrong, sir—this is perhaps the greatest that can be rendered me.

(Emmanuel leaves.)

BERTRAND

(who has risen and gone to the side of the Emperor)

Sire!

EMPEROR

What do you want, my old friend?

BERTRAND

Sire, less than an hour ago, Your Majesty said to me, "Tell me what you wish, Bertrand and if it is in my power to fulfill your desire what you ask me is granted in advance—in the name of my wife and child."

EMPEROR

It's true, I said that. Well, that do you wish, Bertrand?

BERTRAND

I want Your Majesty to give me one of the two rings that you bear on your fingers—that is to say—half the poison Emmanuel is preparing.

EMPEROR

To do what?

BERTRAND

To die on the day the Emperor dies.

EMPEROR

Bertrand—you have a son; you have a daughter.

BERTRAND

Both are rich, thanks to the kindness of Your Majesty—both can get along without me.

EMPEROR

Bertrand, you are mad.

BERTRAND

Sire, Your Majesty is free to refuse me this poison, but as was said just now, there is always the Pistol of Beaurepaire at hand.

(going to throw himself on his bed.)

EMPEROR

It shall be as I promised—go—let that console you.

(General Michel enters, then the Duke of Vicenza.)

EMPEROR

Well—

GENERAL MICHEL

Sire, the gravity of the news I bring to Your Majesty must excuse my presence.

EMPEROR

Speak, sir.

GENERAL MICHEL

Sire, Blücher and his 60,000 men are no longer before us—what we thought was his army was only a screen to hide his movements—Blücher left yesterday at six o'clock and is marching on Paris.

EMPEROR

On Paris?

GENERAL MICHEL

Yes, Sire, through Nogent and Provins. He has ten hours' start on Your Majesty. In three days he can be before Paris.

EMPEROR

(throwing himself down on his bed)

The Duke of Vicenza! Let them call the Duke of Vicenza. The army on its feet. We leave in ten minutes for Paris.

(Vicenza enter)

Ah, Caulaincourt—it's you. Come. You are returning to Châtillon.

DUKE

My powers, Sire?

EMPEROR

You have carte-blanche, sir. Save the honor of France—that's all I insist on.

DUKE

But for yourself, Sire—what shall I demand? What shall I exact?

EMPEROR

Nothing. Napoleon will never depend on anyone except Napoleon.

(The Duke leaves.)

EMPEROR

(writing)

And now to Joseph, "My brother, in conformity to the verbal instructions I gave you, and to the spirit of all our letters, you must not, in any case permit the Empress or the King of Rome to fall into the hands of enemy. You will be several days without news of me—if the enemy advances on Paris in such strength that resistance will be useless, then have the Regent, my son, the ministers, and other dignitaries and the Treasury depart in the direction of the Loire. Don't leave my son—and remember, I'd prefer to know he was in the Seine than fallen into the hands of the enemies of France. The fate of Astynax has always seemed to me the most wretched in history—Napoleon—" But who will take this letter? In whom can I have complete confidence? Ah, Bertrand, my friend.

BERTRAND

Sire—?

EMPEROR

Bertrand, wounded as you are, you must leave instantly for Paris—to take this letter to my brother, Joseph. You understand? to him and no one else. Bertrand, this time, it's more than my life that must be saved—it's that of my wife and my son. Go, go, my friend, while the communication by way of Villeneuve and Coulommiers are still free. Go! But what are you waiting for—speak!

BERTRAND

Sire, I'm waiting for the ring.

EMPEROR

Well—then take it. Bull head.

(gives it to him. To Emmanuel)

Follow your uncle, sir—you will answer to me for his life—to horse gentlemen to horse.

BLACKOUT

ACT II
SCENE 5

The Court of the Polytechnical College.

At rise, the students are exercising with muskets and cannon.

MAJOR

(in charge)

Cannoneers—to your weapons. March! Halt. Front! Action! Charge! Break ranks.

(In stacking the weapons Henry allows the butt of one of them to fall on Arthur's foot.)

ARTHUR

Clumsy!

HENRY

What do you mean, clumsy?

ARTHUR

Don't you see you put your gun butt on my foot?

HENRY

Really. Why did you put your foot under my gun butt?

ARTHUR

Why! Why!

HENRY

Ah, you are really delicate, dear friend, you need to work on that, you see.

ARTHUR

I'd really like to work on you—how's that?

HENRY

In what way?

ARTHUR

This veteran's tone you take displeases me. Gentleman of the second year.

HENRY

Well, if my tone displeases you, you must say so.

ARTHUR

Well—I am telling you.

HENRY

And?

ARTHUR

I repeat what I told you.

HENRY

Can it go on for long like this?

ARTHUR

Time puts an end to all things.

HENRY

Anyone got a ruler? Here's a gentleman wants me to take his measure.

LEON

(from inside)

Well—what's going on down there? A fight?

ARTHUR

Oh—it's only a lesson in mathematics.

LEON

Oh—look—what are you thinking about? Henry! Henry?

HENRY

It wasn't I that went looking for this fight. It's this gentleman who's upset on the pretext they crushed his foot with a gun butt and that the butt refuses to apologize.

LEON

Come on, come on. Peace.

ARTHUR

You are going to give me the pleasure of touching you up, right?

LEON

Look, Henry, you—who are more reasonable—

HENRY

I'm not angry with him.

ARTHUR

Oh—were not so nasty as we seem, Mr. Veteran.

HENRY

Say, say—do you think I shrink from it—by chance?

ARTHUR

No—but I say after graduating the college you must go into the munitions corps. That's a corps which makes more noise than work.

HENRY

Ah! That's how you want it! Here!

(striking him)

En-garde, now!

ARTHUR

Room! Room! Gentlemen, he has insulted me—

HENRY

Touche!

ARTHUR

Nothing; nothing—a scratch on the hand. A handkerchief and let's get on with it.

VICTOR

(entering)

Well—what's going on here? A fight—comrade against comrade? Frenchmen against Frenchman—when the Prussians are at the gates of Paris.

ALL

The Prussians? Impossible.

VICTOR

Impossible? Here—look at this proclamation. Citizens, a

column of the enemy has crossed the Maux. It is advancing on the road to Germany—but the Emperor is closely following it.

ALL

Long live the Emperor!

VICTOR

The Regency Council has seen to the safety of the Empress and the King of Rome. I am staying with you.

HENRY

What does it mean—the safety of the Empress and the King of Rome—?

VICTOR

Gentlemen—the Empress and the King of Rome left Paris this morning at eleven o'clock.

ARTHUR

Left—the Empress? Left?

VICTOR

She didn't wish to—but she was forced to. The King of Rome didn't want to leave the Tuileries—he let out horrible screams—his governess was obliged to carry him in her arms—Now, here's what I have done. I thought it my duty in your name to offer our services to the minister of war.

ALL

Bravo! Bravo! Well—the Minister—?

VICTOR

Impossible to get to him. I didn't want to come back here but to stay at the barricades—but it seemed to me that would be a betrayal of you, my friends.

ARTHUR

Right, Victor!

VICTOR

Here then is the way things stand. If they're going to fight to defend Paris—shall they fight without us?

ALL

No.

VICTOR

In that case, let's take arms.

ARTHUR

Comrades, comrades, you know—the orders are very precise. A student must not leave the campus without permission. All disobedience is punished by eight days in confinement.

VICTOR

Well—there's a way that no one will be punished.

ALL

Which is?

VICTOR

That everyone disobey.

LEON

Comrades, I understand. I partake of your enthusiasm, but remember, we are the sons of officers and we must—

VICTOR

It's precisely because we are the sons of officers that we must defend our country—and if you fear—

LEON

Oh—don't think that, Victor and I will prove to you that like anyone else I know how to earn a captain's bars on the field of battle.

VICTOR

Good! Moreover, the Emperor's brother is making an appeal to all Parisians.

HENRY

We owe everything to the Emperor. He formed the school. We want to defend Paris and die for the Emperor.

ALL

Long live the Emperor. To muskets—to cannons—to arms and now—open the gates—break down the gates.

MAJOR

(entering.)

No. need.

ALL

The Major.

MAJOR

Here are the keys. I authorize you to leave—for in a case like this one would have to be a poor Frenchman to oppose your ardor.

ALL

Long live the Major.

MAJOR

If I were not chained here by orders, I would not let anyone else have the honor of leading you toward the enemy.

ALL

Bravo! Bravo!

MAJOR

Go, kids, go. And may I have the joy that not one of you will fail to be here at next roll call.

VICTOR

Those who don't make it, Major, you will find at the Invalides on the Pantheon. And now, cannoneers, to your cannons—you to the Barricades at Blouche and the bluffs of Saint-Chamont—and we will go to the Barricades at Clichy.

(They leave shouting, "Long live the Emperor!")

CURTAIN

ACT II
SCENE 6

The Barricade at Clichy.

Great tumult at the barrier. The toll keeper frets as if it were an ordinary situation. A cart is brought in by a peasant.

PUBLIC CRIER

Here is the Proclamation of King Joseph—Lieutenant General of the Emperor and Commandant of the National Guard to the Citizens of Paris—one sou! Here's the Proclamation.

A MAN

Give it here, my friend. Give it here. Here, anybody—I am going to read this.

SPECTATORS

Read that to us—read us that.

(The Crier can be heard as he goes off.)

VICTOR

(entering with students from the school)

No need, no need! As the proclamation announces: "As the enemy is before us—we are going to the enemy."

ALL

Bravo! Bravo! The École of Polytechnic is with us. Long live the École Polytechnic.

AIDE DE CAMP

(entering)

Watch out, watch out!

VICTOR

What news, sir? What news?

AIDE DE CAMP

There's fighting on the hills of Saint-Chamont—the Duke De Ragusa is at Romainville.

(cannon fire)

Do you hear—? That's him firing now—watch out—watch out!

(He leaves.)

PEASANT

They need us more than the wounded.

VICTOR

There they are.

ARTHUR

Hello, Father Clopen, hello, Father Clopen.

WOUNDED

Hello Greenhorn.

ARTHUR

Ah, you say that because you do things in the grand style.

SOME VOICES

Hey! The National Guard. Long live the National Guard.

(While they fraternize center stage, a regiment of the line arrives.)

VICTOR

The Line! The Line! Ah, it's you, Lorrain. My father! Where is my father?

LORRAIN

It's more than a week since we saw him. He must be resting somewhere, poor Colonel.

VICTOR

And where is that, my friend?

LORRAIN

Damn—where three quarters of the regiment are—where the

final quarter will lie—sleeping on this big camp bed called a battlefield.

VICTOR

Dead, my father, dead.

FORTUNIO

(entering)

Alive, very much alive, Mr. Victor—set your mind at ease.

VICTOR

Ah, it's you, Fortunio?

FORTUNIO

Yes, Mr. Victor, and here's my sister, Catherine Michélin—whom you know, and what's more, my nephew, Napoleon Michélin—whom I have the honor to present to you.

(Pointing to the child tied to his knapsack.)

VICTOR

Hello, my good Catherine. Things turned out okay?

CATHERINE

Yes, Mr. Victor—wonderfully—as you see.

VICTOR

So that the child—

FORTUNIO

The child is recognized and the proof is that I bear him on my back so he won't tire poor Catherine out—

VICTOR

But say, in a retreat it's not very prudent.

FORTUNIO

Depends how your beat a retreat, Mr. Victor. As we never show our backs to the enemy the child is always safe.

VICTOR

Brave Michélin! Now tell me about my father?

FORTUNIO

Wait—the kid's thirsty. Here Catherine, this doesn't concern me. You're in charge of the liquids department.

(giving her the child)

Your father, Mr. Victor. Here's what it is: the Emperor sent him on a secret mission.

VICTOR

To whom?

FORTUNIO

To His Majesty King Joseph.

VICTOR

Then he's still in Paris.

FORTUNIO

He's in Paris.

VICTOR

How can it be. I haven't seen him?

FORTUNIO

How long has it been since you left the L'École?

VICTOR

More than an hour.

FORTUNIO

Well—there you see he must have been forced to take the back way—and cannot have arrived until last night or this morning—the roads are not safe. And your sister?

VICTOR

She is safe with my aunt in Rue Hilder.

BERTRAND

(from the wings)

The 24th Regiment of the Line? Isn't it here that the 24th regiment is mustering?

VICTOR

I'm not mistaken—it's his voice. Father! Father!

BERTRAND

(entering)

Victor, my child.

(changing his tone)

Why have you left the school, sir?

VICTOR

They let us leave to fight, father—and I thought the only voice to listen to was that of France. France called "To Arms!" Father I took up arms and here I am.

BERTRAND

You have done well, sir.

VICTOR

Heavens, it's you, Emmanuel, Surgeon Major! Plague. You don't waste any time.

EMMANUEL

It's a favor that I don't owe to my merit, Victor, but to the bounty of the Emperor.

VICTOR

And the Emperor is still good to you, Father?

BERTRAND

Before leaving him, I asked for the only thing I deserved and he granted it to me. But that's not the question. My friends—I am your commander.

SOLDIER

Long live Colonel Bertrand! Long live the Colonel.

FORTUNIO

Present, Colonel.

BERTRAND

Friends, it's simply a question of dying here—are you read to do it?

LORRAIN

All that you do, we will do, Colonel.

SEVERAL VOICES

The Enemy! The Enemy!

BERTRAND

Come—charge! Forward. Give them once and for all indigestion from lead and steel.

FORTUNIO

Tie up the kid.

(They replace the child on the knapsack.)

BERTRAND

(to the men of the people)

And you, my friends, defend the barricade. It's a poor fortification, I know, but the true wall of a city is in the heart of its children. Forward! Forward!

(The cannon comes closer. A fusillade can be heard not two hundred feet from the barrier. The men of the people shout 'to the barricade'.)

MONCEY

Retreat, my friends, retreat! Occupy the heights—defend the barricades—without that, by God, you will be cut to pieces. Requisition the houses—fire from the windows.

(to Colonel Bertrand)

What regiment?

BERTRAND

The 24th, Marshall.

MONCEY

Colonel Bertrand, then—

BERTRAND

Yes, Marshall.

MONCEY

Good! I'm not needed here since you are here. You promise to defend this barricade?

BERTRAND

To the death!

MONCEY

That's perfect. My aides de Camp will bring you my intelligence and return with any you have. I'll be at the Barricade Blouche. Make way, my friends, make way!

(Exit Moncey.)

BERTRAND

Come on, barricade the gate, quickly boys—quickly. Catherine, give a drink to all these folks—I'll pay.

CATHERINE

Oh—there's no need of that Colonel. They know very well that on battle days—distribution is gratis. Drink boys, drink.

(to Fortunio)

Well—how about you?

FORTUNIO

I'm keeping the canteen.

(takes it and drinks)

Good—there's not enough to refresh a chicken in your cask.

CATHERINE

(lighting grenades with cannon wick and hurling them)

Cursed grenades, get out!

AIDE DE CAMP FROM THE NATIONAL GUARD

What's the matter with your grenades?

VICTOR

Sir, I don't know what it is—but just now more than a third misfired. Someone must have betrayed us to give us such munitions.

AIDE DE CAMP

No one betrayed you—do you understand, sir—! And if your grenades don't work, it's because you don't take care with lighting them.

VICTOR

I think you're mistaken, sir—if the grenades don't work, it's because they are stuffed with flour and ashes.

AIDE DE CAMP

If the grenades don't work, sir, it's because you light them badly.

VICTOR

And I light them badly because?

AIDE DE CAMP

Because you were frightened they would blow up in your hands.

VICTOR

Because I'm afraid, you say?

BERTRAND

What? Who said Victor was afraid?

VICTOR

Nothing father, nothing.

(Victor takes a grenade in each hand and puts them under the nose of the Aide de Camp.)

VICTOR

Here, sir, you cannot say they are badly lit, right, well of two perhaps only one will blow.

AIDE DE CAMP

What the devil are you doing? Throw those grenades—throw them for God's sake!

VICTOR

Damn, you say I'm afraid.

(The Aide de Camp makes the grenades leap, by giving a blow to each of Victor's hands. Only one of the grenades explodes.)

BERTRAND

(growing pale)

Oh—the Wretch!

AIDE DE CAMP

Receive my apologizes, sir.

VICTOR

That's not the point.

(A fusillade can be heard in the wings. Reply by rifle shots. A shell falls on the stage.)

ALL

Watch out for the shell.

(They scatter—they throw themselves flat on the ground. The fusillade stops.)

VICTOR

Look out!

(He rushes to cut the wick.)

BERTRAND

(pulling him away)

My turn.

(The shell explodes. Bertrand puts his hands over his face.)

VICTOR

Father!

EMMANUEL

Uncle!

(pulling Bertrand's hands from his face)

Fresh water with drops of eau-di vie. This will be nothing—
hardly a wound.

BERTRAND

Then I can stay at my post?

EMMANUEL

After you are treated, Uncle.

(They lead Bertrand into a house.)

VICTOR

Listen, Catherine, do me a big favor.

CATHERINE

Two, Victor.

VICTOR

Run to the Rue Hilder—inform my sister that our father has been slightly wounded, do you hear—do not frighten her. I may be sent elsewhere—Emmanuel has his duty—my father may be abandoned. Let her come as quickly as possible with a carriage—we will take father in it—go!

CATHERINE

Fortunio, they recommended the child to you.

FORTUNIO

Get going—he's there in his hammock.

(The fusillade begins again. Then the trumpets announce a truce bearer.)

SEVERAL VOICES

A Truce bearer! A truce bearer.

(They open the gate of the barricade.)

A MAN

Any enemy truce bearer! Fire on him.

AIDE DE CAMP

Stop, gentlemen—a truce bearer is sacred. Let him in. I am

going to find the Marshall.

FORTUNIO

(to the truce bearer)

Wait there, Captain.

CATHERINE

Fortunio! Fortunio. Here's Miss in person.

FORTUNIO

Eh, Colonel—Colonel—here's Miss France.

BERTRAND

(leaving the house)

France, my daughter.

CATHERINE

Father! Father! Don't take off the bandage. Emmanuel order him not to—

FRANCE

Father—are you wounded?

BERTRAND

It's nothing—my face is a little burned by powder, that's all. Emmanuel says in a week you won't be able to notice.

FRANCE

Really true, Father?

BERTRAND

(taking the bandage in his hands)

My oath—!

EMMANUEL

(trying to stop the colonel from taking off his bandage)

Uncle!

VICTOR

Father!

BERTRAND

Oh, so much the worse! It's nearly a year since I saw her—I have to see her—France, my daughter—

(tearing his bandage)

Where are you so I can look at you at my ease?

FRANCE

Why, I'm right here, Father.

BERTRAND

You are there? I touch you—I don't see you. Oh, misfortune!

Misfortune! My eyes are burned. I'm blind.

FRANCE

Father.

VICTOR

Father.

EMMANUEL

(to France)

Take him away—take him away right now.

FRANCE

Come, come, Father! Our love will sustain you despite all—even as light from heaven—Come, come!

(She leads the Colonel out.)

MONCEY

(entering)

Where is the truce bearer?

TRUCE BEARER

I'm here, Marshall.

MONCEY

What do you want?

TRUCE BEARER

To treat for the capitulation of Paris.

MONCEY

Who are you coming from?

TRUCE BEARER

On behalf of Prince Schwarzenberg.

MONCEY

Return to the Prince and tell him that when it's a question of capitulation, he must address himself to someone other than Marshall Moncey.

TRUCE BEARER

That's your last word, Marshall?

MONCEY

Yes, sir, go.

ALL

Long live Marshall Moncey!

MONCEY

Long live France.

(firing begins again.)

Everyone to his post—and may it not be through the barrier at Clichy that the enemy enters Paris.

(The action continues. The barricade is broken by Prussian cannon fire. The French counterattack fiercely. Tableau—the Barricade of Clichy.)

CURTAIN

ACT III

SCENE 7

An Inn at Avignon.

Porters drinking and singing. Emmanuel is seated at a table.

PORTER

(singing)

Madam Ango's corset is not the same as the Corsican from Corsica—for the Corsican from Marengo is the toughest corset around.

POINTU

Shut up—shut up—you sing out of tune like an osprey.

PORTER

Say, Pointu, is it true you fired this cannon ball which turns the spit at Loulle?

POINTU

Take it off and give it to me—you will see.

LA CALADE

Will you leave my cannon ball alone? Well good—and the spit—
don't you have to make it revolve like the sun for everyone?

POINTU

It's true! The Corsican has fallen—it's a feast. Come, wine,
wine!

LA CALADE

Oh, if you want to drink to the fall—the cellar is for you.

POINTU

You've got it in for him, too? The ogre of Corsica?

LA CALADE

Didn't the gendarmes take my fiancé six months ago? And
wasn't he shot under the pretext that he had deserted with
weapons and baggage?

POINTU

Really—you are charming—let me hug you. Hell, come on you
guys—here's the place to drink, eat, and dance.

(The bring in some wine. Drums—cards—dancing.)

PORTER

(running)

Hey, guys—say—do you know—?

ALL

No, but tell us, we want to know.

PORTER

They're escorting him to Elba and he's coming this way.

ALL

Who's that?

PORTER

Nicolas, then!

POINTU

The Corsican? The Corsican is passing this way?

PORTER

What are you saying?

POINTU

I say you're mistaken; he's not coming this way.

PORTER

What—he's not coming this way?

POINTU

No—he's stopping here.

ALL

Understood; understood.

LA CALADE

If he must fall here, I insist on being part of it.

INNKEEPER

What? A murder? What are you thinking of, wretched woman?

POINTU

Hey Cook—mind your own business or if not, the River is nearby.

EMMANUEL

(rising and going to him)

Put it there, comrade.

POINTU

You are one of us?

EMMANUEL

Yes, and in any event, if he avoids Avignon, we are in Aux.

POINTU

No need—here's an axe that will do his business.

ANOTHER

Here's a bayonet which only waits for its moment.

LA CALADE

And here's a knife, which is not broken. I pride myself on that.

POINTU

(to Emmanuel)

And you, I don't see any weapons?

EMMANUEL

(pointing to his pockets)

I have them there, in their kennels—two bull dogs that bay and kill at the same time.

POINTU

Good! I see you are brave.

(The noise of a carriage is heard.)

ALL

What's that? What's that? A carriage. That's him. To the carriage! To the carriage!

(They run out.)

EMMANUEL

(remaining to the Innkeeper)

You are an old soldier.

INNKEEPER

Well, what of it?

EMMANUEL

You do not make common cause with those brigands.

INNKEEPER

One is not an assassin, that's all.

EMMANUEL

You were in the First wars?

INNKEEPER

Who told you that?

GENERAL MICHEL

I did.

INNKEEPER

My old brigade commander. You remember Papa Moulin?

GENERAL MICHEL

Yes, as a brave and faithful soldier of the Emperor—so—can we count on you?

INNKEEPER

Yes—yes—but quiet! They're coming back.

(Enter Pointu, Captain Campbell, Major Koller, Porters—the crowd.)

CAMPBELL

Well, gentlemen—what's this all about—and what do you want?

POINTU

We want the Usurper.

CAMPBELL

These folks are mad.

POINTU

What did that redcoat say?

PORTER

He says we are mad.

CAMPBELL

Mad or rabid, as you choose. Where's the owner of the hotel?

INNKEEPER

That's me, Captain.

CAMPBELL

I am the English Commissioner charged with escorting the Emperor Napoleon to the Island of Elba—and here's my colleague, the Prussian Commissioner—Mayor Koller.

PORTER

The Emperor Napoleon.

(murmurs)

CAMPBELL

Yes, gentlemen, the Emperor Napoleon. One does not cease to be Emperor because he no longer lives in the Tuileries—any more than the Pope who died at Valence ceased to be Pope because he no longer lives in the Vatican. All Majesties come from on high. Who was—is—and who is, will be!

PORTER

Well—he won't be much longer—that's all I have the honor to tell you, Mr. Commissioner.

CAMPBELL

Aren't there any authorities in charge of this town?

POINTU

Oh yes, the authorities—but the authorities require strength.

CAMPBELL

Is there no garrison here?

POINTU

Two hundred men—troops of the line.

CAMPBELL

Two hundred men have a commander?

MONTAGNAT

Yes, sir, I am the Commandant.

(Murmurs.)

CAMPBELL

I need to speak to you, sir.

MONTAGNAT

And I was looking for you. I wanted to ask you, sir, if His Majesty, the Emperor has an escort sufficient to make a courageous resistance in case of attack?

CAMPBELL

Do you fear an organized attempt?

MONTAGNAT

Some wretches have sworn that the Emperor will not leave Avignon alive.

POINTU

What are they whispering about?

CAMPBELL

Gentlemen, leave us this room, if you please.

POINTU

What! What! This room—that is the common room—anyone can stay here if he eats or drinks. Wine, Papa Moulin, wine.

(He sings.)

Madam Ango's corset is not the same as the Corsican from Corsica—for the Corsican from Marengo is the toughest corset around.

CAMPBELL

(to the Innkeeper)

My friend—give us a private room.

POINTU

Hey, where are they going?

CAMPBELL

If you have the right to remain in the commons—we have the right to take a private room.

INNKEEPER

Go in, gentlemen—that's my sister's room.

CAMPBELL

(taking a lamp)

Come, gentlemen.

(He leaves with Koller and Montagnot.)

POINTU

That's okay—plot as much as you like—he's got to pass this way and we're ready for him here.

GENERAL MICHEL

(to Emmanuel)

What's to be done?

EMMANUEL

I think the only thing is to die with the Emperor.

GENERAL MICHEL

Then let's signal our friends.

EMMANUEL

Let me go find them; they don't suspect us.

GENERAL MICHEL

Oh—you won't have to go far—they are there in the gateway.

(Emmanuel goes to the door, opens it and sees the street full of people.)

EMMANUEL

(aside to General Michel)

Let's reunite and hold ourselves in readiness.

(aloud to the others)

Don't worry, friends, he won't be long in getting here.

(Pointu has been listening at the door and trying to see through the keyhole.)

POINTU

Hush! There they are! There they are!

(The Commissioners returns.)

CAMPBELL

Make way, gentlemen, if you please!

POINTU

Well—have we made our little plans? Are we going to save the great man, eh?

CAMPBELL

We hope so, gentlemen. Make way!

(He leaves with Koller and Montagnot.)

(La Calade comes out of the same room.)

LA CALADE

Hush!

ALL

La Calade!

LA CALADE

Come here! I know everything. We are going to get the brigand!

EMMANUEL

(aside)

What's she going to say?

LA CALADE

I was in my room when they came in, I blew out the candle, and hid myself behind the curtains. Here's what they plan to do. The Emperor won't stop here.

ALL

Huh?

LA CALADE

He will go round the city and change horses at the Gate of Saint Lazarre.

POINTU

Is there a post change at the gate of Saint-Lazare! The post horses are here. He's got to come here.

EMMANUEL

Commandant Montagnot has undertaken to find some horses.

POINTU

Well then—let's go to the Saint-Lazare gate.

ALL

(rushing from the house)

To the Saint-Lazare gate.

EMMANUEL

(after watching them leave and get out of earshot)

Papa Moulin, we must save the Emperor?

INNKEEPER

How to do it?

EMMANUEL

While they go to wait for him at the gate of Saint-Lazare, run to the main highway. The first carriage which passes will be his. The Russian and Austrian commissioners are with him. You will stop the carriage—you will tell the Emperor what has happened and bring him here by some private door.

INNKEEPER

But what if he doesn't believe me?

EMMANUEL

You will tell him that it is I, Emmanuel de Mérigny. who sends him this advice. Here General, here Colonel—go with Mr. Moulin—I—I'll wait here with these gentlemen.

(Noise of the carriage.)

EMMANUEL

Silence.

ALL

What?

(The Emperor appears.)

EMMANUEL

The Emperor, gentlemen—the Emperor. he hasn't had time to be warned—and what should have ruined him—saves him. Come, there's always a star in heaven for him.

(After the Emperor enters, they draw the curtains. The Emperor is accompanied by the Allied Commissioners, and Major Koller enters.)

EMPEROR

Well—what do you say, my dear fellow? That the Avignois wish to assassinate me? I thought they must be satiated after the massacre of the Glacier—who are these men?

EMMANUEL

Sire, servants devoted to Your Majesty and ready to die for you.

EMPEROR

Ah! Emmanuel de Mérigny—thanks, sir! It's good to find people one loves and esteems on route to exile.

CAMPBELL

Sire, is there some way we can do you good in the danger you run?

EMMANUEL

Gentlemen, you can have the horses put on your carriage by saying who you are and by announcing that His Majesty follows you in a third carriage. Go gentlemen, and think whose existence you are charged to protect.

(The Commissioners leave.)

EMPEROR

It's really you, Mérigny? It's really you, General Michel? But there's another good friend I don't see among these gentlemen, that's Colonel Bertrand. Could he have been killed?

EMMANUEL

No, Sire. He wasn't that lucky.

EMPEROR

Is he dead?

EMMANUEL

No, for he's unaware of Your Majesty's abdication.

EMPEROR

He's unaware of my abdication? Did it cause so little stir in France that a single Frenchman is unaware of such an event?

EMMANUEL

Sire, Colonel Bertrand is blind.

EMPEROR

Blind! My poor Bertrand!

EMMANUEL

An exploding shell burned out his eyes.

EMPEROR

Oh! What you say there! At least he is rich?

EMMANUEL

Yes, Sire, thanks to the goodness of Your Majesty.

EMPEROR

Blind! What a misfortune.

EMMANUEL

Yes, doubtless, but God has given us a consolation in the misfortune.

EMPEROR

Which is?

EMMANUEL

That, thanks to the terrible accident, we've been able to hide from him the fall of Your Majesty—a fall of which you know quite well, Sire—he did not wish to survive.

EMPEROR

Yes, you said it Mr. de Mérigny—the hand of God was in this misfortune—but you've joined together with some purpose.

EMMANUEL

With the purpose of saving you, Sire.

EMPEROR

How's that?

EMMANUEL

As Your Majesty can see, your life is running the greatest danger.

EMPEROR

Oh, sir, in my twenty years of war, I've seen death so close that a very real danger must present itself for me to salute it. Anyway, I can say like Shakespeare's Caesar—danger and I are two lions born the same day—and I am the elder.

EMMANUEL

Well, so be it, Sire—never mind the danger however great it may be. Let's think of the future.

EMPEROR

Of the future?

EMMANUEL

Yes, Sire! six leagues from here, on the other side of the river between Caumont and Saint Audeal ten men are waiting for us—nothing could be easier than to carry you off and to reach the Gulf of Lyon. There, the brother-in-law of General Lallemand, a Captain of long duration is waiting for you with his brig—you go abroad, he hoists sail and you go to America to await events.

EMPEROR

America! That's much too far.

EMMANUEL

Your Majesty is then determined to go to the Island of Elba?

EMPEROR

Yes. Mr. de Mérigny, can I personally do something that will be agreeable to you?

EMMANUEL

I will ask the Emperor the privilege of accompanying him in his exile.

EMPEROR

It's a sad privilege—but I am accustomed to the devotion of your family—it is granted. You will be surgeon major of the guard. Well—what's that noise?

(The Commissioners and the Innkeeper enter.)

CAMPBELL

Sire—the rumor has spread that Your Majesty is here. The people who were at the gate of Saint-Lazare are blocking all the exits to the house. They won't let the carriage leave—they threaten to cut the traces of the horses—they threaten—they still threaten the life of Your Majesty.

EMPEROR

Well, sir?

EMMANUEL

We are here, Sire, ready to die for you and with you.

CAMPBELL

Yes, gentlemen—but we are charged with the protection of the Emperor—no harm must come to the Emperor—it would be a bloody stain on the heraldry of the four powers.

EMPEROR

(very tranquilly)

Then, gentlemen—it seems to me it's up to you to find a way.

CAMPBELL

Sire, if Your Majesty will consent to put on this coat, this hat, if Your Majesty consents to pass for a person in our suite.

EMPEROR

Come on, gentlemen!

EMPEROR

Sire, Sire—in the name of heaven

(shouts outside)

Sire, think that we have to respond for you.

EMPEROR

(shrugging his shoulders)

To whom, sir?

CAMPBELL

To the world, first—then to God.

EMMANUEL

(rushing towards the door pistols in hand)

Gentlemen you know what we have to do.

EMPEROR

Enough! I consent. I don't want a single drop of blood shed for me.

(he puts on an Austrian uniform)

Open.

(They open the doors and windows—the people rush in.)

THE PEOPLE

Where is he? Where is he?

CAMPBELL

Whom do you want, gentlemen?

POINTU

It's not you we've got it in for.

CAMPBELL

Who is it then?

POINTU

The one they call the Emperor.

COMMISSIONER

He's not among us.

POINTU

'Cause, if he were, you see—

EMPEROR

(coming forward)

You would kill him mercilessly, right?

ALL

(raising their arms)

Without mercy!

EMPEROR

(removing the Austrian uniform—first the hat, then the coat—
then with perfect calm)

Then strike. I am the Emperor.

ALL

The Emperor! The Emperor!

(All arms fall—all rage abates.)

CAMPBELL

Oh, Sire,—only Your Majesty can perform such miracles.

EMPEROR

Haven't you heard it said, sir, there are men who pet tigers and who tame serpents? It's a matter of looks—that's all. To carriage gentlemen, to the carriage.

POINTU

(pushing people aside, axe in hand)

Make way for the Emperor. And if anyone touches him—he'll have to deal with me.

BLACKOUT

ACT III
SCENE 8

Colonel Bertrand's home in Grenoble—a room giving on the garden with a kind of terrace.

Victor is writing at a table. France is leaning on his shoulder.

FRANCE

Have you finished?

VICTOR

Yes, dear sister—here's the day's news.

FRANCE

And what's all this other bundle that I've seen you working on for nearly a week.

VICTOR

Listen carefully to this, dear sister—it's the advance work in preparation for a voyage which perhaps won't have to be made.

FRANCE

For a voyage?

VICTOR

Yes—it is possible I may be forced to absent myself for a couple of weeks—for a month—for two months perhaps.

FRANCE

For two months? You, Victor, leave us, leave my father?

VICTOR

Nothing is less certain then this voyage, France, and now as I tell you about it—it is becoming likely in certain eventualities. Well—here for two months, day by day the news that you can read to my father. I don't need to tell you, do I, dear sister, in case I am obliged to leave—to watch over him for both of us— not to let anyone come near him unless this person is warned that father is unaware of all our misfortunes.

FRANCE

Don't worry—from the moment we began to deceive poor Papa, it has become necessary to deceive him to the end. But where are you going?

VICTOR

You will excuse me, won't you, France, if I refuse to tell you?

FRANCE

So it's a secret?

VICTOR

Yes.

FRANCE

You are leaving?

VICTOR

I am going to take a tour of the coast of Sicily with my musket.

FRANCE

You won't be angry with me, Victor, if I tell you that for some time you've worried me?

VICTOR

No, but I would ask you where this worry comes from?

FRANCE

Victor—we are living in a time when—you'll admit, there's something to fear, isn't there?

VICTOR

For what reason?

FRANCE

For political reasons. They know the attachment of our family to the Emperor—the government is suspicious.

VICTOR

Well—

FRANCE

Well, Victor—these hunting parties at Mathesines, in the Jouffré Valley—in the lakes of La Fray—these excursion which last two or three days—these frequent absences in the past, this even longer absence you threaten us with in the future—Victor, I'm afraid you are mixing in these conspiracies of which we hear talk of all the time. Victor, I'm afraid you are conspiring!

VICTOR

Hug me, France.

(France hugs him)

You are crazy—

(He takes his rifle and leaves.)

FRANCE

Poor father—this is all he would need—if he learned at some time that the Emperor, his God, is no longer on the throne and that my brother is conspiring. Then there would be two reasons to die instead of one. Oh, that ring he wears on his finger and which contains poison—if I could get him to give it to me—or at least, if he could be separated from it for a minute.

PIERRE

Miss—the Prefect of Isére.

FRANCE

Have him in.

PIERRE

Come in, Prefect, sir, come in.

PREFECT

Pardon, miss, if I present myself in this way in your home.

FRANCE

Come, sir, come.

PREFECT

I would like to speak to you, to you or to your brother.

FRANCE

My brother went out, sir, but I am here.

PREFECT

Can you grant me a few minutes?

FRANCE

Certainly, sir, anyway, my father is here—and if you will excuse me.

PREFECT

No, thanks, what I wish to tell you—to you, miss, or your

brother—must be done, on the contrary, in the absence of the Colonel.

FRANCE

Please take a seat, sir; I am listening.

PREFECT

Miss, is not unaware that in a time like ours, four months after the fall of a man whose destiny is tied to so many diverse interests, that, however broken, remain living—seeking to rejoin—in conspiracies and plots.

FRANCE

I am listening, sir, but I don't understand.

PREFECT

I am going to explain more clearly, Miss. The administration has received from Paris the strictest orders—you will do me justice to say that despite my nomination to the prefecture of Isére, I've done as much as was in my power to soften them.

FRANCE

Yes, sir, I know you are very highly regarded, much loved in this territory.

PREFECT

Well, Miss—strange things have come to my attention so you will not be surprised that I have come to you for an explanation. They tell me that the Emperor fallen for all the world, remains on the throne for the Colonel. That pretended victories are told to him—and strange orders given. They've told me, among other things, that it's pretended that he is the military commandant and that under this pretense, and under the pretext that yesterday was the 15th of August—the Day of Saint Napoleon—he uttered some kind of proclamation in which he invited the inhabitants of Grenoble to illuminate their windows.

FRANCE

Alas, sir—it's a long and sad story that you ask of me.

PREFECT

No matter, Madame, tell it.

FRANCE

My father owes to the fallen one his fortune, rank. My father believes he hasn't sacrificed to him all that he owes him. At Méry-sur-Seine, the Emperor—pardon—he who was reigning then—almost perished in the midst of a party of Cossacks. My father saved his life. Ten minutes later, the man whose life my father saved, realizing that all was lost, that at any moment he might fall into the hands of the enemy, had my cousin, Mr. de Mérigny—a surgeon, prepare a poison subtle enough so he could always be master and commit suicide. Then my father rising and approaching the Emperor, demanded as reward for saving his life—one of two rings filled with this poison—swearing to die not only if the Emperor did but even if he ceased to reign.

PREFECT

You are right—miss. That's more than devotion—that's fanaticism.

FRANCE

Sir, you know, in what glorious circumstances my father lost his sight—but Paris was taken. The empire collapsed and Napoleon fell with it—the condition of my father was not the worst misfortune we were threatened with—my father had taken an oath not to survive the fall of his benefactor.

My father has never failed to fulfill an oath. But he must be brought to betray this one. So it was, sir, that my brother had the idea of making my father believe that Napoleon returning from Fontainbleau arrived in time, beat the allies before Paris and pushed them back to the frontier and remains master of France and on the throne. The thing was easy because of the misfortune which befell him. My father was born at Grenoble—we had kept some friends who were ready to assist us in this pious ruse. They simulated a Brevet from the Emperor in reward for his service—naming my father the military commandant of this territory. We brought him here, set him up in this house where he was born, and which is less strange to him than any other—for he can see it with the eyes of memory. Then, established here, we surrounded him with a sort of cordon sanctum so that no stranger could reach him. Every day, my brother prepares the news which we read to him. Bulletins the victories Napoleon has sent from an imaginary battlefield and my father, forgetting everything, even though he no longer sees us, in thinking his benefactor not only is not dead, not only is not a prisoner, but is still victorious, all powerful, and supreme master of the destinies of Europe. It's a dream, sir, but my father is living because of and by means of this dream. Don't let him be killed by reality.

PREFECT

So, you think, Miss, that if your father, despite all precautions, were to learn the truth—?

FRANCE

Oh—God is my witness, sir, I more than once treated our lie as a betrayal thinking what violence would happen to him if this second bandage was torn from his eyes. Then the truth rose from my heart and from my lips. But as soon as my eyes fixed on that ring he wears on his finger—on that ring which contains death—and as long as I see that ring on his hand, I dare tell him nothing.

PREFECT

So—that's the truth, Miss?

FRANCE

Oh—Sire, the pure truth—complete. Anyway here he's coming. Because of his misfortune, he won't notice your presence. Stay here. Look, listen and you will leave convinced.

(Bertrand enters leaning on Fortunio's arm.)

BERTRAND

Ah, my brave Fortunio, say we gave them another roughing up at Montmédy?

FORTUNIO

Yes, yes—I got that from Mr. Victor who read it in the public papers—and that they almost took Blücher's brigade.

(noticing the prefect)

Huh?

BERTRAND

What's wrong?

FRANCE

(going to him)

Nothing, father. Fortunio thought I was in the garden and noticing me, he was astonished—that's all.

BERTRAND

Well, knowing you are here, I am happy—come my child—come!

FRANCE

Fortunio, my father doesn't need you any more since I am here—go about your business.

FORTUNIO

(aside)

What's this stuffed shirt doing here? Hum! It will bring us misfortune—that's my way of thinking.

BERTRAND

Where is Victor?

FRANCE

He took his rifle and went hunting, father.

BERTRAND

Have you seen the paper?

FRANCE

Yes, father.

BERTRAND

Read me news of the army—

(France unfolds the paper and shows the Prefect the paper prepared by Victor.)

FRANCE

"The Army Corps of Marshalls Trevise and Ragusa, reinforced by a part of the Army of Lyon—commanded by His Majesty, the Emperor, met the Army Corps of Marshall Blücher and General Sachem at Montmédy—the engagement began at seven in the morning and lasted until eleven—at eleven the enemy was in full retreat—he left 2,000 men on the field of battle and six cannons and twelve hundred prisoners are now in our hands—"

BERTRAND

Good! And the Bulletin? Isn't there a bulletin?

FRANCE

No, father, that's all there is. "The Empress assisted yesterday at the representation of the Opera, and was greeted on her entry into her box with shouts of 'Long Live The Emperor! Long live Marie Louise'."

BERTRAND

Fine! Thanks, my child! Thanks my little Antigone. Look at the injustice of historians, my dear child—you have done for me more perhaps, than the daughter of Oedipus, but as my name is an obscure one, it drags your name into my obscurity. What are you doing?

FRANCE

I'm looking at this ring, father.

BERTRAND

Leave it alone, leave it alone, France, that ring must never leave my finger.

FRANCE

Oh, father, if I asked you nicely, if I went down on my knees, if I said to you—"Father, I am jealous if this ring that never leaves your finger—Father, give me that ring."

BERTRAND

First of all, my child, I will begin by saying there is nothing in the world of which you ought to be jealous—since there is nothing I love more than you, although it is more than a year since I've seen you, your memory is always there and in the obscurity in which I walk, your face is the only object which remains clear and visible to me—like that of an angel—ask whatever you want of me—but don't ask this ring of me.

FRANCE

And if this ring is all I want, father?

BERTRAND

You will renounce it when I tell you this ring is a gift from the Emperor, and especially where, in place of this ring, I will give you an object much more valuable.

FRANCE

What, Father?

BERTRAND

Here, take this medallion.

(pulling it off)

It's a portrait of your mother. Alas! I can no longer see it. Only when I touch it, I remember this other angel who is gone ahead to heaven to mark the place you must occupy one day. Take it, and look at it often—you can see it—so that after having been a girl as you are, you may be a good mother like she was. Take it and leave this ring, my child.

FRANCE

Father!

BERTRAND

Take me back to my room, France.

FRANCE

Will you let me have Fortunio escort you? I have to stay here for a few minutes. In five minutes I will be with you.

BERTRAND

Do that, my child, do that.

FRANCE

(calling)

Fortunio!

(to Prefect)

Well, sir?

PREFECT

You are a saint, Miss! Let me speak to your father. I want to add my little bit to your security by associating myself with this pious lie.

BERTRAND

To whom are you speaking, my child?

FRANCE

Father, it's the territorial Prefect that Fortunio has just brought in. And he wants to speak to you.

BERTRAND

Have him in.

FRANCE

He is here, Father.

PREFECT

Hello, Colonel.

BERTRAND

Mr. Prefect—

PREFECT

You won't think it bad, Colonel that charged with the civil administration of the department, I want to talk with you who are charged with the military command?

BERTRAND

On the contrary, sir, I'm happy for this opportunity. Only—you understand, Mr. Prefect, the Emperor decided to reward my services more than I deserve—I am titular head, that's all—my infirmity.

PREFECT

A glorious infirmity, sir!

BERTRAND

My infirmity precludes all detail work. It's my son who does everything. I sign the reports he presents me and I ratify the orders he gives.

PREFECT

That's why, sir, I came to put myself directly at your disposition. By marching in concert, Colonel, the civil administration will work better with the military. But you were getting up, sir—you were going back to your room—I won't stop you.

(Fortunio appears.)

BERTRAND

Nonsense, Mr. Prefect.

PREFECT

I, myself am in a rush. I hope to give orders relative to Saint Napoleon.

BERTRAND

Yes, that's tonight. You read my proclamation?

PREFECT

The invitation to light up? I read it.

BERTRAND

I hope the victory at Montmédy will be a new stimulant to the patriotism of the townsmen. We are in the country of liberty, sir,—it is here it took its birth.

PREFECT

(smiling)

I notice that perfectly well.

(low to France)

In your turn—are you happy with me, Miss?

FRANCE

Thanks, sir—you've done more than I dared hope.

PREFECT

Colonel—to the honor of seeing you again.

BERTRAND

Prefect—

(The Prefect bows and leaves.)

FORTUNIO

(aside)

What did he mean? Is he in it, too? The stuffed shirt.

BERTRAND

You are there, Fortunio?

FORTUNIO

Present, Colonel.

BERTRAND

Well, come and give me your arm.

FRANCE

No need, father—let me escort you.

BERTRAND

And what you had to do?

FRANCE

I will do it later, later—but at the moment, I prefer not to leave you.

BERTRAND

You have the medallion?

FRANCE

Here, around my neck, where it will remain forever.

BERTRAND

Fine! Come child.

(He leaves, accompanied by his daughter.)

VICTOR

(entering from the garden)

Fortunio.

FORTUNIO

Ah, it's you, Mr. Victor.

VICTOR

Tell me—what's it mean? The Prefect—

FORTUNIO

Eh! My God, yes—he left, Mr. Victor.

VICTOR

Left here! And what did he come here for?

FORTUNIO

Oh, that's the question. What did he come here for? No bad thing it would appear since he told your sister she was a saint— that's my way of thinking.

VICTOR

And to my father? Did he speak to my father?

PREFECT

Yes, he told him he was going to give orders apropos de Saint Napoleon.

VICTOR

Do you understand all this, Fortunio?

FORTUNIO

No, but your sister can explain it all to you.

VICTOR

Doubtless, but later—but, right now, I haven't the time. Some friends are coming to meet me here. I am expecting them.

FORTUNIO

You know that meetings of more than twenty persons are forbidden.

VICTOR

We are only five or six. Anyway, we are not conspiring, Fortunio.

FORTUNIO

You are not conspiring? So much the better. Anyway, everyone is free to keep their secrets—but in any case, if you are conspiring beware of the tricolors! The tricolor is their nightmare. They are capable of shooting my dog if they meet it on the street with a tricolor cockade hanging from its ear. Why should that be? Because they know, you see, he will return, one day or another. Also I have mine hidden, stitched in my police bonnet—and I sleep with it—it never leaves me, day or night.

VICTOR

That's fine! That's fine! Fortunio, you will bring rum and lemonade—it's a bachelor party—we need punch—don't mention this little debauch to anyone—not to my father—and even less to my sister.

FORTUNIO

That's understood. Anyway, you are the second master of the house when the first is absent. Free in every respect—Mr. Victor. That's my way of thinking.

VICTOR

Listen, Fortunio.

FORTUNIO

Present.

VICTOR

I am expecting the friends I've spoken of by the garden gate. As this gate gives on a little deserted street, and as our house is a little suspect they prefer to enter that way—they will knock three times like this, d'you see? Rap! Rap! Rap! Stay by the garden gate and open it. When these gentlemen get here you will be relieved of duty.

FORTUNIO

Fine.

VICTOR

Then bring the rum and lemons and then you can go to sleep. As we will have no further need of you. Wait—it seem to me they're knocking. Yes, go, open.

(General Michel, the Colonel and other officers seen at Avignon with Emmanuel—they are disguised as hunters and muleteers.)

VICTOR

(to himself)

This visit by the Prefect disturbs me—as soon as my friends are gone, I will see my sister and find out—ah—here's someone.

COLONEL

(on the stone steps)

Are you alone, Victor?

VICTOR

Yes—don't worry—you can enter. No one has seen you.

COLONEL

No one! Come in, gentlemen.

VICTOR

How long have you been here?

COLONEL

Since yesterday morning—these gentlemen since this evening.

FORTUNIO

The company is assembled. Right, Mr. Victor?

VICTOR

Yes.

FORTUNIO

Well, here's the lemonade, the rum—sugar and all the kit and caboodle.

VICTOR

Thanks, my friend.

FORTUNIO

Say, Mr. Victor.

VICTOR

Well?

FORTUNIO

I don't say you're conspiring, but no matter, take care you don't let yourself be taken—eh?

VICTOR

Go! Go! Don't worry, my friend!

FORTUNIO

You understand—it's my way of thinking—

VICTOR

Right.

(Exit Fortunio.)

VICTOR

We are assembled, gentlemen. Let's proceed quickly and without losing a minute. Let each of us say what he has done and we will see what remains for us to do.

COLONEL

I am coming from Cambrai. I've seen General Lefevre-

Desnouettes who commands the Royal Chasseurs—meaning, the Chasseurs of the Imperial Guard—he's going to talk with the Count d'Erlon and both will join forces on the day agreed, moreover, I passed through La Fère, I saw Lallemand—he answers for seizing the Arsenal, and returning, I conferred with General Rigaud at Châlons—he's waiting for your communication.

GENERAL MICHEL

I saw Count d'Eilon—he commands the garrison at Lille. He undertakes to march on Paris at the first signal. He answers for his men as himself. And you, Victor?

VICTOR

I undertake to raise the whole territory of Isére. There's not a peasant with a musket who is not at my disposition.

GENERAL MICHEL

Well—I will give you news. This King is furious. Everywhere there is a Vendee plot, an ultra conspiracy. It's a question of nothing less than a Bonapartist St. Bartholemew.

COLONEL

Have you seen the secretary of state?

GENERAL MICHEL

Yes.

ALL

Well, what does he think?

GENERAL MICHEL

He thinks that the moment has come from the Emperor to make a bold attempt.

VICTOR

And he gave you a letter of introduction to the Emperor?

GENERAL MICHEL

No—he told me that a word from him found on one of us is death. But at the time he left the Emperor, as sign of recognition the Emperor tore in ten pieces a letter from the Empress Marie Louise as a sign of recognition. Each piece is a talisman which must conquer the confidence of the illustrious prisoner to whoever presents it. One of these precious fragments was confided to me—and here it is.

ALL

Fine! Fine!

GENERAL MICHEL

Now—who is going to leave for Elba?

ALL

Me! Me! Me!

GENERAL MICHEL

Pardon gentlemen—we are all so devoted to the Emperor that the choice of one of us would be an injury to the others. Anyway, my opinion is that in great affairs, Fortune must be left its role.

Let's put six names in a hat. Whoever's name is drawn will be our messenger.

ALL

Very good idea.

GENERAL MICHEL

Is it agreed?

ALL

Completely.

GENERAL MICHEL

Let's write, gentlemen.

(each writes and places a folded paper in a hat)

Who will draw?

VICTOR

Gentlemen—would you like it to be a man completely foreign to our situation? The old soldier who let you in, for example?

GENERAL MICHEL

Marvelous.

ALL

Yes! Yes! Yes!

VICTOR

Fortunio! Fortunio!

FORTUNIO

Say, good thing I didn't take the opportunity to go to sleep like you told me to, Mr. Victor.

VICTOR

Yes, my friend. Come and put your hand in this hat—pull out a name—it's a lottery.

FORTUNIO

It seems I am playing the role of cupid. There.

GENERAL MICHEL

Let's see—

(opening)

Victor Bertrand.

FORTUNIO

Ah—you won the big lottery, Mr. Lieutenant.

VICTOR

Thanks, Fortunio, thanks, gentlemen.

GENERAL MICHEL

Do you need money, Victor?

VICTOR

No, General, I have all that is necessary.

COLONEL

How about a passport?

VICTOR

I have a passport for Turin. Once in Turin I won't have to worry.

GENERAL MICHEL

Let's go, old fellow—good luck!

ALL

Good luck, my dear Victor!

(They embrace him.)

VICTOR

I will do my best, gentleman, don't worry. Fortunio—escort these gentlemen out, I am on my way in two hours.

GENERAL MICHEL

God watch over you.

(They leave.)

VICTOR

(alone)

Thanks beautiful harlot called Fortune—hopefully this time you've loved a man worthy of you, the Emperor! See the Emperor—bring him the oaths of an entire nation—to be intermediary between France and him! And if he ever again puts his foot on the throne, hand on his scepter, and says to me, says to me that I made him take this step into the future, to write this great page for history. Oh—succeed or die, my name, the name of my father will be a name not lost to posterity. Now a word to my sister, my poor France.

A pen, ink and paper.

(writing)

My dear France, I am leaving. Don't ask me where I am going. I am going to take my share in a great work. I don't know if you will see me again, but whether you see me again or not, from this moment the nation, our beloved mother, will be proud to count me in the number of its children. I commend you to our father. Your brother, Victor.

FRANCE

(has come forward and read over Victor's shoulder)

Give it to me, brother.

VICTOR

You were there?

FRANCE

Yes, I saw disguised men enter through this gate and I was uneasy. I came down. I won't ask you what you are going to do or where you are going. I say to you, brother: be careful—brother, take care of yourself for your sister and your father.

VICTOR

Dear France, listen: I see you are worthy of knowing everything—I see you are of an ancient race. France, I don't wish to have any secret from you. Tonight I am leaving for the Isle of Elba.

FORTUNIO

(who has entered)

For the isle of Elba!

VICTOR

Ah! You heard did you?

FORTUNIO

Don't pay attention, Mr. Victor, it fell on deaf ears. Only take care as I told you: don't let yourself be taken.

VICTOR

I will do my best. Don't worry. In any case, the bets are placed. Come sister.

(He leaves with France.)

FORTUNIO

(looking at the untouched wine bottles)

He calls that a debauch! Trust this to me.

BLACKOUT

ACT III

SCENE 9

The terrace of a house inhabited by Napoleon at Porto Ferraio.

The Emperor is with Captain Campbell.

EMPEROR

Yes, surely, sir, England is a great nation and the proof is that my eternal policy—that to which I owe my situation here—was to ruin England. But France, believe me, has, in the future, a much more providential mission than England.

CAMPBELL

Providential, Sire? Then why did God, despite your expensive weaponry, protect France so ill against England—why have you only Taillebourg and Fontenoy to oppose to?

EMPEROR

Oh! Speak boldly, sir to Poitiers, Crécy, and Trafalgar.

CAMPBELL

Sire, it is you who named these English victories.

EMPEROR

Defeats from which it was thought a country would never recover. And now, sir, France is still on its feet. The English always beat us, but we always kicked them out. It's true the English burned Joan of Arc and would like to treat me worse. But they'd better watch out. The French made Joan of Arc a Saint. The English need only to make me a martyr in order for the French to make me a god.

CAMPBELL

By making yourself immortal in advance, you've spared them most of the trouble.

EMPEROR

Touche, sir. Still, what causes this national hate that for six centuries exists between our people? Like Rome and Carthage—why did Carthage succumb rather than Rome? Was Scipio greater than Hannibal? No. It's because Rome had an idea—a civilization—huh—someone wants me?

GRAND MARSHALL

May I have a few words with Your Majesty?

CAMPBELL

Sire, excuse me.

(He goes off.)

EMPEROR

I will keep you for dinner, Captain.

CAMPBELL

I shall be at Your Majesty's orders although you treat my poor England very ill.

EMPEROR

The plaintiff who loses his case has three days to curse his judges—the case I've lost was long enough to give me a year.

CAMPBELL

And after a year?

EMPEROR

Who knows? Perhaps I'll file an appeal. Go, sir, go.

(Campbell leaves.)

EMPEROR

(to Marshall)

Well, what's wrong?

GRAND MARSHALL

Sire, there's a young man disguised as a sailor just come from the inn and was busy changing clothes when they went to his room to ask the purpose of his trip. He answered he had come to see Your Majesty and gave his name—which is, in fact, that of one of the bravest imperial officers.

EMPEROR

And his name is?

GRAND MARSHALL

Victor Bertrand.

EMPEROR

Very well—I remember—I even have by me one of his cousins, our Surgeon Major de Mérigny. And you say he asks to see me?

GRAND MARSHALL

Sire, they brought him without giving him time to change clothes.

EMPEROR

Have him come.

GRAND MARSHALL

Here he is, Sire.

(Victor enters.)

EMPEROR

Come forward, sir.

VICTOR

Sire.

EMPEROR

You are coming from France?

VICTOR

Yes, Sire.

EMPEROR

To do—you bring me some news?

VICTOR

Sire, I think it's good.

EMPEROR

Your name?

VICTOR

Victor Bertrand, Sire.

EMPEROR

You are a relative of Colonel Bertrand?

VICTOR

I am his son.

EMPEROR

You are the son of a brave and loyal soldier, sir. If I had had only ten men like him around me, things would have happened differently.

VICTOR

Oh—nothing is lost, sire.

EMPEROR

Really?

VICTOR

To the contrary!

EMPEROR

You didn't see anyone before leaving Paris, Sir? You don't bring me any sign of recognition.

VICTOR

Here's my response, Sire.

(He presents him a paper.)

EMPEROR

A fragment of a letter from the Empress—be welcome. You have seen the Secretary of State?

VICTOR

No, Sire, but he judges that all is ready in France for Your Majesty's return, and he sends you this sign.

EMPEROR

Well then, speak, sir.

VICTOR

Sire, the honor Your Majesty has done me by admitting me to His Presence troubles me so much that I would prefer that Your Majesty questioned me. I will reply.

EMPEROR

Is it true? There is discontent in France?

VICTOR

Oh, Sire, since Your Majesty no longer commands the French, they seem to understand all they have lost.

EMPEROR

Yes, when I reigned they condemned me—while today they value me—they offered me Italy as a price of my abdication. I refused. When one has reigned in France, one doesn't need to reign elsewhere. Look—what do my soldiers say about me?

VICTOR

Sire, they ceaselessly discuss your immortal victories. They never mention your name without admiration and regret. When the Bourbons give them money they drink to your health—and when they force them to shout long live the king, they add under their breath "of Rome."

EMPEROR

Then they still love me?

VICTOR

More than ever.

EMPEROR

What do they say of our misfortunes?

VICTOR

They look on it as the effect of treason. They say that you were never beaten—you were betrayed.

EMPEROR

They're right. If Paris had held out a day longer, the Allies would have been defeated. I had isolated them from their supplies—not one of them would have escaped. I had all Europe with me.

VICTOR

It won't be that way today, Sire. Today France knows what she's worth: if attacked she will triumph as she triumphed in the great days of the revolution—for your misfortunes have taught her that armies do not suffice to save a nation while a nation that rises completely is always invincible.

EMPEROR

The opinion I was forming of France is exactly the same, I see that. And Bassano, you say, is of the opinion this cannot go on much longer?

VICTOR

Yes, Sire—his opinion on this point agrees with popular opinion. He adds even that at the first attempt on your part.

EMPEROR

(quickly)

France will receive me as a liberator?

VICTOR

I'll answer for that, Sire.

EMPEROR

Would you advise me to return, sir?

VICTOR

Sire, I am almost a child—and wouldn't dare utter an opinion in such a matter—but I do not hesitate to say to Your Majesty that I have come to put at your feet—in the name of our most famed generals and colonels, the expression of a unanimous, universal, immense desire—the desire for your return.

EMPEROR

You are right. When they hear the report of my name, they'll be afraid. I will unfurl the tricolor to my grenadiers. I will appeal to the memories of those they send against me. The army will not fail to welcome me, for I covered it with glory. Come, come—I no longer hesitate. Leave, return to France—see my friends— tell them to talk—to fortify by every possible means the good morale of the people and the army.

VICTOR

How shall I leave, Sire?

EMPEROR

One of my ships is taking sail for Naples—go with it—your father is at Grenoble?

VICTOR

Yes, Sire.

EMPEROR

It's on my way to go to Paris. Before the 15th of April I will shake his hand. You will remember all I have told you.

VICTOR

Oh, I didn't miss a single word of Your Majesty—and first to last, they are all engraved in my memory.

EMPEROR

I am going to prepare your letters. Return about nine o'clock on this terrace. Today, is a feast day on the island. I'm giving a ball and fireworks—till we meet again, sir, till we meet again. I will send you instantly to Mr. de Mérigny. Whatever happens not a word about the purpose of your trip.

VICTOR

I will obey, Sire.

(The Emperor leaves.)

Oh, I've seen the Emperor—I've really spoken to him. Oh, I understand very well the enthusiasms of these men who would die for him—ah, I understand my father's fanaticism.

EMMANUEL

(appearing on the terrace)

Victor! Victor!

VICTOR

Emmanuel.

EMMANUEL

My brother, my dear Victor! And the Colonel?

VICTOR

Marvelously well.

EMMANUEL

France?

VICTOR

She's waiting.

EMMANUEL

Dear beloved. Ah, if she knew that of all things—she is all that I regret.

VICTOR

She suspects it.

EMMANUEL

But how did you get here? How were you able to obtain a passport? You must have had a thousand difficulties?

VICTOR

I came by way of Turin—and as I didn't have a passport—I took the place and outfit of a sailor.

EMMANUEL

And the purpose of your trip?

VICTOR

To put myself at the disposition of the Emperor—to take service under him, if by chance he has need of me.

EMMANUEL

You've seen him? What did he tell you?

VICTOR

He told me to wait for his orders on this terrace.

(Catherine and a solder enter.)

CATHERINE

Say, Mr. Victor, can anybody have a word with you?

VICTOR

Ah, Catherine—I should think so. Are you happy, Catherine?

CATHERINE

Yes, Mr. Victor—as much as one can be—who is a widow before becoming a wife. But I have around me men who love me—anyway, I see you alert, looking well, gay—and Miss France—the Colonel, Fortunio, himself—are they all well?

VICTOR

Yes, Catherine—all are well—and all think of you, too.

CATHERINE

You know, I met a brave lad named Lorrain who was near Jean when he fell—Lorrain says Jean was not dead when he last saw him. It gives me hope.

(The natives of Elba in feast costume enter.)

NATIVES

(entering in a crowd)

The Emperor! The Emperor! Long live the Emperor!

EMPEROR

(entering)

Thanks my friends.

(to Victor)

Here are your letters, sir. Your boat—Go! Go!

(Victor kisses the Emperor's hand and leaves)

EMPEROR

(to his suite)

Come, gentlemen, to the fireworks.

LORRAIN

Excuse me, Sire?

EMPEROR

What is it?

LORRAIN

Sire, today is a feast day on Elba—and consequently to some extent Your Majesty's as well—that gave us an idea—to make a little gift to our Emperor.

EMPEROR

You! A gift! Ah, kids—!

LORRAIN

Yes, Sire—and one that won't displease you—at least so I think—all right everybody.

(Drumbeats—troops appear and arrange themselves in battle order. An older soldier comes forward with a flag over a portrait of the King of Rome.)

LORRAIN

Port arms! Present arms!

(Military music—the portrait is uncovered.)

ALL

Long live the King of Rome.

EMPEROR

My son—my friends! Oh—you are right. The gift is great and worthy of you. But how did you do it?

LORRAIN

We wrote Mr. Talleyrand, who is at the Congress of Vienna.

EMPEROR

My son! My son! Oh, I will restore the throne of France to him.

SHOUTS

Long live the Emperor!

(Fireworks go off.)

CURTAIN

ACT IV

SCENE 10

A room in the Colonel's house in Grenoble.

The Prefect is escorted in by Fortunio.

PREFECT

That's fine, my friend. That's fine—only warn the Colonel's daughter I need to have a short conversation with her.

FRANCE

(entering)

Here I am, sir. I saw you come in and I ran.

FORTUNIO

(aside)

I am going to warn Mr. Victor that the stuffed shirt is here.

(Exit Fortunio,)

FRANCE

Pardon, sir, but the honor your visit does us, is always mixed—
much as you have reassured us—with a certain uneasiness.

PREFECT

And you are wrong, Miss; for I can tell you that your filial devotion has made you a friend of mine.

FRANCE

Sir—

PREFECT

And I am come to give you a proof—an unexceptionable proof,
Miss—for if what I am going to tell you does not remain between
us, I will be gravely compromised.

FRANCE

You've come to demand my silence?

PREFECT

I have the right to demand it and to insist on it, even, in return
for the service I am going to render you.

FRANCE

Speak, sir.

PREFECT

You know the motive of my last visit?

FRANCE

Yes, sir—and I thought you left convinced.

PREFECT

Of the ignorance and good faith of the Colonel—yes, miss—I have no doubt remaining on that subject, but—

FRANCE

But—?

PREFECT

But it is not so, with regard to your brother.

FRANCE

With regard to Victor?

PREFECT

With regard to Mr. Victor, yes.

FRANCE

My God! You scare me, sir—although we have no reason—

PREFECT

Your brother took a trip?

FRANCE

Yes, sir.

PREFECT

A two-month vacation?

FRANCE

Two months, yes.

PREFECT

He left on that trip the very day that I paid you my visit?

FRANCE

I no longer recall—I think—

PREFECT

I am sure of it; he's been back for a month.

FRANCE

Yes.

PREFECT

Well, a report has been made to me about that trip. They assure me that your brother was entrusted with a message for the King of Naples.

FRANCE

Oh, sir, I swear to you.

PREFECT

Miss, I have the honor to tell you for the second time, it is not the Prefect who comes to you, it's a friend who fears for your family. So long as the Prefect is not forced to see, he will be as blind as the Colonel—but consider carefully, Miss, such blindness pushed too far may become treason.

FRANCE

Well, sir, what do you want? What do you want? I don't know what to say.

PREFECT

What I want, what I intend, miss, is for your brother to consider himself worried that his conduct is suspect—that he be aware denunciations have been made against him. I know quite well that denunciations must be scorned and you see I more than scorn them since I denounce the denouncers—but if these same denunciations are made in Paris—if—I—I receive an order—whatever it requires, I'll have to execute that order—once arrested, your brother won't belong to me anymore, he'll belong to the law—tribunals are severe in times of civil war like ours and—

FRANCE

Sir, oh! I recognize your conduct towards us is really that of a friend. Well, that's not all—having told us the danger you must tell us how to avoid it—my brother arrested! Victor before a count martial! Truly, you render me mad with terror. What must he do? What must we do? Speak! Speak!

PREFECT

I repeat, I have not received an official order; if I had received it, I would be forced to obey it—well, in the freedom of action which I retain, the advice I have to give your brother, the advice of a friend, of a father, is—is to leave instantly—without waiting for night to come—to leave Grenoble—it's not far from here to the bridge of Beauvoisin—and he knows the way.

FRANCE

Sir—

PREFECT

Remember, I cannot say, and consequently have not said—it's you, you alone in your sisterly solicitude , who will give him this advice—remember—

FRANCE

Silence, sir, silence!

(Bertrand entering came in hand, groping about.)

BERTRAND

France!

PREFECT

I shall retire—

FRANCE

Father?

PREFECT

You were talking with the Prefect.

FRANCE

Me? Who told you that?

BERTRAND

I recognized his voice. You know quite well that, through the goodness of Providence the other senses succeed, those senses one has lost. I recognized the voice of the Prefect. Where are you, sir?

PREFECT

Here I am, Colonel.

BERTRAND

Ah, I knew it!

(to France)

Hug me child and leave us.

FRANCE

What—leave you? Why, father?

BERTRAND

Because I have business to discuss. What is surprising for the military governor and the Prefect to confer together about governmental things? Go, my daughter, go.

FRANCE

I will retire, father, since you wish it.

(low to Prefect)

Permit me to remain. I am very uneasy.

(After a sign of agreement from the Prefect, France goes to the Prefect, opens the door, then closes it, but remains on stage.)

BERTRAND

I was going to beg you to come see me.

PREFECT

Me, sir?

BERTRAND

Yes, take advantage of my infirmity, don't I? Eh! I would prefer to be able to go to you—but, let's get back to what I have to tell you. What! His Majesty, the Emperor is going to visit our department and I knew nothing of it! The Emperor is coming to Grenoble and I was not forewarned of it.

PREFECT

The Emperor?

FRANCE

(aside)

My God!

BERTRAND

Yes, it was a surprise they wanted to give me. Oh! I have bad eyes, but good ears. I cannot see, but I can hear.

PREFECT

You hear?

FRANCE

(aside)

What has he heard?

BERTRAND

Yesterday, Victor was talking with his sister and didn't see me.

PREFECT

Pardon, Colonel, but what Mr. Victor said to his sister was perhaps secret and I haven't the right—I, a stranger.

BERTRAND

It was a secret, but a secret we both must know, you as a civil official, I, as the military commander. Well, Victor said to his sister that Spring would not be over without the Emperor being here—at Grenoble.

FRANCE

Father!

BERTRAND

Oh, you are there! They disobey me on the pretext I cannot see. Are you going to tell me I heard wrong?

FRANCE

Yes, yes, you heard wrong, father, for what Victor said was only a probability, less than a probability—a supposition—my brother supposed—

BERTRAND

He didn't suppose, Miss—he said, "I saw the Emperor and the Emperor told me—"

FRANCE

Father! Oh, silence in the name of heaven. Mr. Prefect.

PREFECT

I certainly said, Miss, that it was a secret, a very grave secret and one which consequently ought to remain in the family. As for me who learned it without wishing to learn it, I declare to you, Miss, that it is as if I didn't know it. Tell we meet again, Miss. Goodbye, Colonel.

(Exit Prefect, France runs to a table and writes.)

BERTRAND

Well, what's got into him, our Prefect? Ah yes, I understand. He didn't even know of this resolve of the Emperor—of crossing Dauphin—on his return from the campaign—and I let it out like a pistol shot at close range. Well, where are you France?

You are writing, I think. To whom?

FRANCE

No, father, I am not writing.

BERTRAND

I hear the pen scratching on the paper.

FRANCE

You are mistaken, father.

BERTRAND

It's possible. But I am not mistaken in thinking that something strange is going on here. Your voice is choked—heavens- your hand trembles.

FRANCE

Yes—I am thinking to what degree Victor will be disappointed. He wanted to hide from you this news of the passage of the Emperor through Grenoble. It was a secret that the Emperor had begged him to keep.

BERTRAND

And does he think I will keep this secret less well than you? Does he think his father is less discreet than his sister?

FRANCE

Father—you told this news to the Prefect. Well, well—this secret is no longer a secret.

BERTRAND

Ah—if that's the way it is, you are right, my daughter—yes, and I am the one who is wrong. Why didn't you tell me that? Do you suspect my devotion to the Emperor?

FRANCE

Oh, no, no, father, on the contrary. Everyone knows you are ready to die for him—they know—oh, but for that, but for that.

BERTRAND

Come, come, it seems I've committed a big blunder.

VICTOR

(entering)

France.

BERTRAND

Eh?

VICTOR

Nothing, father—I've come back and I wanted a word with France.

BERTRAND

A word with France? And on what subject?

VICTOR

I'm having two or three friends to dinner, father, and I would like France to have us served in this room, if you permit—

BERTRAND

Take this room—take the dining room—take the whole house, but for God's sake don't let me be scolded any further by your sister. I leave you to make your preparations. Goodbye, my children.

FRANCE

Bye, papa.

FORTUNIO

Here I am, Colonel—file to the left—forward—march!

(Fortunio exits with the Colonel.)

FRANCE

You heard?

VICTOR

Yes.

FRANCE

Well, not a minute to lose.

VICTOR

To do what?

FRANCE

To depart, to leave France.

VICTOR

I can't do that without having seen our friends again.

FRANCE

But you will be ruined if you remain.

VICTOR

I will be ruined if I leave. I have a rendezvous with them in ten minutes. I will warn them and we will flee together but alone, no—that would be cowardice—treason.

FRANCE

Let's see—which way will they come in?

VICTOR

Why as usual by the garden gate.

FRANCE

Well, if I were to wait for them? If I were to tell them?

VICTOR

No, not you, but Fortunio. Your place is by our father—at the risk of our lives he must be unaware of everything—go up to his room—go up—send me Fortunio.

FORTUNIO

(entering)

Present!

VICTOR

I expect some gentlemen—the same who came the last time.

FORTUNIO

They are familiar.

VICTOR

Go place yourself as a sentinel at the garden gate—and when they arrive, tell them 'All is discovered. Flee.'

FORTUNIO

Understood—it shall be done.

VICTOR

(to his sister)

You are still here?

FRANCE

Do you need me, brother?

VICTOR

No, I have everything necessary. Go stay by father—go.

FRANCE

Victor.

VICTOR

France! Poor France. I will have better days.

FRANCE

Listen, it seems to me someone is knocking on the door.

VICTOR

Which one?

FRANCE

The street door.

VICTOR

Go, stay by father, I tell you! That is important—go!

(He pushes her out.)

VICTOR

Let's see—anything missing? No—money—I have some weapons—right here—here's my passport—a cloak—Well, France was not mistaken they are knocking at the street door. Not an instant to lose.

(He rushes out only to meet General Michel.)

VICTOR

You, General! Fortunio didn't warn you?

GENERAL MICHEL

Indeed, but I wanted to know the extent to which we've been compromised.

VICTOR

They know of my trip to Elba. That's all. But you and our friends are not suspected.

GENERAL MICHEL

Never mind, we are all answerable.

VICTOR

If you trust me, general, let's leave. They're knocking at the street door and I fear they may be armed.

GENERAL MICHEL

Let's leave. Let's leave.

AIDE DE CAMP

(coming in)

It's too late.

VICTOR

What did Fortunio do, then?

AIDE DE CAMP

It's not his fault—he warned us—but both ends of the street were guarded.

GENERAL MICHEL

Let's fight it out! We are six and well armed.

FORTUNIO

Pardon, general—we are seven—at least that's my way of thinking.

(Prefect enters followed by Gendarmes who remain at the rear.)

PREFECT

Mr. Victor Bertrand, in the name of the King, I arrest you.

VICTOR

Pardon, sir, but will you have the goodness to give me some explanation?

PREFECT

I don't have to give any, sir, but nonetheless, I will. In returning home just now, I found an order from Paris to arrest you as a conspirator.

VICTOR

You hear gentlemen.

(He advances towards the Prefect.)

GENERAL MICHEL

(holding his arm)

Halt! Mr. Prefect, I am going to give you some good advice. The next time you undertake a similar mission, take a sufficient force with you. Pistols gentlemen and let's go.

PREFECT

Rebellion against government orders? Gendarmes—do your duty.

GENERAL MICHEL

One step, gendarmes and you are dead.

PREFECT

(gesturing)

Gendarmes, don't fire unless I fall.

(going right to Victor and touching his shoulders)

Sir, you are my prisoner.

COLONEL

(taking him by the collar)

Sir, it is you who are our prisoner.

(Tumult—clash of sabers and the cocking of pistols.)

FRANCE

(entering hurriedly)

Father! Father! He heard some noise—I tried in vain to restrain him—he's coming down—here he is—silence—in the name of heaven or you will kill him.

BERTRAND

(entering)

What do you mean, Victor? You told me there was a reunion of comrades—and from the noise here, one would say there was a quarrel, a struggle, a combat.

FRANCE

No, no, father, take it easy. Only friends are here.

VICTOR

(low to Prefect)

You have an order for me alone, sir?

PREFECT

For you alone.

VICTOR

Then my friends are free to go?

PREFECT

They are.

VICTOR

You have my word, sir, I am your prisoner, but silence.

GENERAL MICHEL

Victor.

VICTOR

(finger on his lips)

Silence.

BERTRAND

(recognizing the voice)

Ah—it's you, General Michel?

VICTOR

Eh, yes father, you see indeed now mistaken you are.

BERTRAND

What? You are in my home, General, and I wasn't informed.

VICTOR

These gentlemen are only passing through Grenoble, father, and they are taking leave of me when you came down—they charged me with all their regards for you—Gentlemen.

(He signals for his friends to withdraw.)

GENERAL MICHEL

Goodbye, Colonel.

THE OTHERS

Goodbye.

BERTRAND

Goodbye.

(Victor makes imperative signals to his friends. The Prefect on his part signals the gendarmes to let them pass.)

FRANCE

And now, father, mercy, please go upstairs.

BERTRAND

(uneasy)

Why Victor! Where is Victor?

VICTOR

Here I am father.

(demands by signs to the Prefect to let him accompany his father. The prefect nods)

Don't worry—I am accompanying you.

(France and Victor escort the Colonel out. The Prefect and the gendarmes watch. Silence. After a minute, Victor reenters.)

VICTOR

Thanks, sir. And now I am at your discretion.

PREFECT

Follow me, sir.

(They all go out except for Fortunio.)

FORTUNIO

I really told him not to let himself get caught.

BLACKOUT

ACT IV
SCENE 11

A chamber in a military caserne at Porto Ferraïo.

Lorrain with a veteran who is mending his shoes.

LORRAIN

(finishing a black circle on an immense calendar on the back wall)

Finished! The 26th of February—

VETERAN

Would you like to say why we are spoiling our imperial calendar like this?

LORRAIN

So I won't mistake the dates. In marking every day, I keep current. Anyway I made a bet with the drum-major.

GOGNAD

What bet?

LORRAIN

I bet a half pound of tobacco with the pouch, that we wouldn't vegetate a year here.

VETERAN

That's why the pompous ass of a drum major pays attention to the farming of tobacco, he's afraid of losing.

LORRAIN

That won't prevent it—if someone wants to go halves with me on my bet, I'll give him a half pound of tobacco for a pound. Ah—now that's business.

SECOND VETERAN

What are you doing?

FIRST VETERAN

I'm putting a tongue in my shoe. That's an issue from Leipzig— it has worked since that time and is overdue for trouble now—worn out—

(opening the flap of his friend's coat)

You really should put grub in your breeches.

SECOND VETERAN

I've been thinking so, too—if only I had a good set.

FIRST VETERAN

Yes, it upsets you to part with them, I know—but what's that on the chair?

SECOND VETERAN

It's a sapper's apron and he is busy preparing food with Catherine. He's afraid of tearing it. Heavens—an idea—! That's my plan—I'll be back.

FIRST VETERAN

Come on—! Does he have a thick skull?

(Catherine enters followed by a Sapper and a Drummer carrying soup in a large cauldron.)

CATHERINE

Watch out everybody—the soup!

SAPPER

(with a big bowl)

Here's the grub. Italian hot cakes, that's all. Fed like Senators, eh!

(He fills bowls ending with his own.)

CATHERINE

(to Sapper)

Why'd you fill this one to the top?

SAPPER

Because it's mine.

CATHERINE

Plague—you cannot refuse anything to your stomachs.

SAPPER

What do you want? I am no egoist.

CATHERINE

Fine! Now the dinner bell.

(she beats on the cauldron with two spoons.)

(The whole barracks come in.)

ALL

Present—Widow Leroux.

CATHERINE

You know very well I don't want to be called Widow Leroux. That brings bad luck to Jean if by some luck he wasn't killed. Well, Lorrain?

LORRAIN

I'm not hungry.

CATHERINE

Oh—if you scorn dinner, decidedly you are very sick.

LORRAIN

France was my mistress as Jean Leroux was your lover. Well, you still regret Jean Leroux. I still regret France—and then—and then—

CATHERINE

And then you're upset with the Emperor—that's the truth.

LORRAIN

Because he behaves worse and worse.

CATHERINE

Heaven—Lorrain, in your place, word of honor, I wouldn't beat around the bush—one fine day I'd tell him to his face.

LORRAIN

He should expect it—he's screwing around with his Island of Elba so as to make me lose my bet—it's childish on his part.

CATHERINE

(to Sapper, who's looking for his apron)

Well—what? What are you looking for, my friend?

SAPPER

I'm looking for my apron.

LORRAIN

Your apron—look! There it's coming.

SAPPER

(to 2nd Veteran)

Well—what's going on? What's going on?

2nd VETERAN

Don't touch. I am repairing—a break—after dinner you'll get your apron back safe and sound.

CATHERINE

Decidedly, Lorrain, you are practicing fasting. Come on—come on.

LORRAIN

Well, just to be agreeable to you, Catherine.

(takes a bowl and eats quickly)

CATHERINE

Get out! It seems to me you are not going badly on the Italian pies for a man who is not hungry.

LORRAIN

I am suffocating sadness.

(filling his mouth)

CATHERINE

Do you know why you are melancholy, Lorrain?

LORRAIN

No, I don't know.

CATHERINE

Well, it's because instead of working on the fortifications, on the mines, you walk around morning till evening with your arms folded dreaming of what has past and cannot return.

LORRAIN

Well, yes, I walk around with my arms folded from morn to evening—well yes, I dream from dawn to dusk—I think of the Pyramids, of Marengo—of Austerlitz and all the rest of it.

Come on—you aren't going to make me believe in all this. Is this a country, I ask you? This button of an island where we are crowded together like oysters on a rock. No—we are poor shipwrecks—not anything else. We are waiting from moment to moment for a ship to take us back to our country. We are crying out. We are here, we are dying, we are eating out our souls. That's what I think. That's what I dream—and that—

(The Emperor, followed by the Drum Major, the Emperor comes in very softly and takes Lorrain by the mustache.)

EMPEROR

And that bores you?

LORRAIN

Tediously, Sire.

ALL

(rising)

The Emperor!

(At the sight of the Emperor, the man with the breaches lets them go. The Sapper follows him to get his apron back.)

EMPEROR

Well—what must be done to distract you?

LORRAIN

I would indeed tell you, but you wouldn't listen to me.

EMPEROR

Never mind—speak out.

LORRAIN

You absolutely want me to?

EMPEROR

I insist.

LORRAIN

Well, if I were Emperor for only five minutes, I would beat the call to arms so that this whole island would tremble.

(The Emperor signals an aide. The aide de camp transmits the sign. Twenty drummers beat the call to arms.)

LORRAIN

Huh? What's that?

EMPEROR

You see—just as you ordered. Continue.

LORRAIN

Ah! Is that all there is to do. Well, I would say 'Fall in— Grenadiers—Port Arms.

(The Emperor makes a sign. From behind the theatre can be heard, "Fall-in, Grenadiers—Port Arms—then further away— Port Arms".)

EMPEROR

Continue.

LORRAIN

Then, I would say goodnight to the cockade of the Isle of Elba and on with the tricolor of France.

(The Emperor makes a sign. An officer empties a cloak on the table full of tricolors.)

LORRAIN

Sonofabitch. That's it!

EMPEROR

Continue.

LORRAIN

Then I would say to the Band—"One of those old tunes which will lead us in a week from Paris to Berlin."

(The band plays, the air "Veillons au salut de L'Empire".)

EMPEROR

And then?

LORRAIN

Well—with that voice which made us pass through fire and ice, I would shout 'To France, soldiers, to France!"

EMPEROR

Well, yes, my friends, to France! To France!

LORRAIN

What, my Emperor—is it possible?

EMPEROR

Yes—possible. We're only waiting for you and your comrades. You're late.

ALL

To arms!

(They throw off their aprons and ready themselves. In an instant, the place is transformed.)

EMPEROR

Well, yes, kids—me too, I was like you. I too was looking at France, I too was waiting. The hour has come. Soldiers, I count, as always, on your courage and devotion. The brig and the boats are waiting. Are you ready?

ALL

Yes, yes.

EMPEROR

Well, whoever loves me, follow me!

ALL

Long live the Emperor!

LORRAIN

Say, Catherine, for the first time, I played Emperor—I hope I didn't play badly.

CATHERINE

Oh—if my poor Jean were here.

EMPEROR

To France! To France!

CURTAIN

ACT V

SCENE 12

The road from Lamon to Vizelle. Some peasants lead a poor devil dressed in torn clothes who seems annihilated with fatigue.

BASTIEN

(to Jean Leroux)

Lean on me. Look, you fellows give him a chair. Well, look, what's wrong with you, my friend?

JEAN LEROUX

I've marched most of the night and I can't go any further.

BASTIEN

Where you coming from? Lyon?

JEAN LEROUX

I am coming from the depths of Russia.

AN OLD WOMAN

From the depths of Russia. Poor dear man! Do you hear Mathieu?

He comes from the depths of Russia.

BASTIEN

Were you a prisoner?

JEAN LEROUX

Yes, wounded at Leipzig and left for dead on the battlefield. Taken with our prisoners to Kiev. Then the peace came and then they told us we were free and that we could return to France. Two or three hundred of our troops started out—and we are about ten left. Fatigue and misery took the others.

BASTIEN

You are from Midi—that's why you came this way.

JEAN LEROUX

No—I am from Saint Dizier.

BASTIEN

Didn't they want you in your country?

JEAN LEROUX

That's not it. I am looking for a young woman named Catherine to whom I was espoused. I learned from her brother she had followed the Emperor to Elba as a vivandiere—she thinks I'm dead.

OLD WOMAN

Well—now there's a brave lad.

BASTIEN

Hey, granny—what do you say? Did they do it like that in your day—when the Romans invaded.

OLD WOMAN

Come on, come on, children—don't speak ill of the past—there were brave men in all periods. So my friend, you really need to eat, drink and sleep, don't you?

JEAN LEROUX

Eat and drink, yes—and start on my way.

BASTIEN

You are really in a hurry?

JEAN LEROUX

Heavens! It's three years since I saw my betrothed and two since I saw my Emperor.

BASTIEN

You are going to see the Emperor?

JEAN LEROUX

I really hope so, unless I lose my sight.

BASTIEN

Well, you tell him hello on behalf of Bastien—of the farm of Grenaux where he slept during the battle of Montemerail. It was a poor bed but he slept well anyway. And there's a fellow with no fear of ghosts. And then you will tell him the farm was burned the evening of that battle and that I've established myself here at Lamure if he should take it into his head to return and—

PEASANT

Hush Bastien.

BASTIEN

Hush? And what's that? Are there spies here? Well—if he should take it into his head to return, he will be welcome—that's all.

JEAN LEROUX

I will tell him—don't worry. Come friends, thanks.

OLD WOMAN

Well—you're going.

JEAN LEROUX

What do you expect? I have to be on my way. Come, goodbye, everyone, granny—

(the sound of a drum)

What's that?

(An avant-garde of the Grenadiers appears)

Really—grenadiers of the guards! I thought they had changed their uniforms.

BASTIEN

Well yes—they did change them.

GRENADIERS

(entering)

Hello, friends, hello.

BASTIEN

Look, they're wearing the tricolor.

LORRAIN

Well, yes, we wear the tricolor—isn't that the National Cockade, for Christ's sake? Yes, we have the tricolor flag. Is it not the Emperor's flag?

BASTIEN

The Emperor's?

LORRAIN

Yes, and as we are the avant garde of the Emperor, Long Live the Emperor!

JEAN LEROUX

The Emperor! The Emperor!

BASTIEN

Is the Emperor really coming?

LORRAIN

He's following us—here's the drum-major who still owes me a half an ounce of tobacco and the drummers and then the Polish Lancers and then the Emperor—and then the Old Guard and then the whole army!

JEAN LEROUX

Then, my friend, you are coming from the island of Elba?

LORRAIN

Straight as a cannon shot.

JEAN LEROUX

Do you know Catherine Michélin?

LORRAIN

Catherine, the Vivandière? Catherine, widow of Jean Leroux? I should say I know her.

JEAN LEROUX

Huh?

LORRAIN

Oh—with honorable intentions. She's our Joan of Arc.

JEAN LEROUX

Where is she?

LORRAIN

A hundred paces back.

JEAN LEROUX

Oh! Catherine! Catherine!

ALL

The Emperor! The Emperor!

EMPEROR

(entering)

Yes, my friends, the Emperor, the Emperor, who, knowing that you miss him, comes with a handful of braves—because he counts on you. You are threatened by tithes, by privileges, by feudal rights, by all the abuses you were freed from by our success. Well, I've come to chase away all your fears—me—the soldier of fortune—the Emperor of the People.

PEASANTS

It's true, Sire, it's true. You come as an angel of the Good Lord to save us. Long Live the Emperor!

CATHERINE

(recognizing Jean Leroux)

Jean Leroux! Jean Leroux! I see you again!

JEAN LEROUX

Catherine!

EMPEROR

What's wrong?

LORRAIN

My Emperor—it's Catherine—she has found her deceased husband.

EMPEROR

That's good, that's good. Let her speak.

CATHERINE

Ah, Sire, it's him—it's Jean Leroux—he didn't die—he was only a prisoner—he's back from Kiev or Moscow. I don't know where! Oh! I am mad with joy!

EMPEROR

And where were you going like this?

JEAN LEROUX

I was going to serve you, my Emperor—I don't know how to live without you, and even less without her.

EMPEROR

Come, gentlemen, some supplies. Clothes for that brave man— and let him retake his rank in my guard.

(to an officer to whom he speaks in a low voice.)

You understand?

OFFICER

Yes, Sire.

OLD WOMAN

Will, the Emperor, be so good as to take some refreshment?

BASTIEN

Well, granny?

OLD WOMAN

Well—what! If the Emperor's thirsty, he must drink.

EMPEROR

Well, yes, granny, I am thirsty—give me a drink.

OLD WOMAN

There—you see.

(She fixes a drink.)

OFFICER

(giving a uniform to Jean Leroux)

Here, my friend.

JEAN LEROUX

Thanks, oh, my brave uniform—I was really afraid of never seeing you again—go!

CATHERINE

Oh! How handsome you are, Jean.

(pointing to a cross on the uniform)

Well—what is that?

JEAN LEROUX

Ah, yes—what is that?

EMPEROR

Well—doesn't the uniform fit?

JEAN LEROUX

Indeed, my Emperor—but it's that—

EMPEROR

What?

JEAN LEROUX

It's that—you see—this little gewgaw.

EMPEROR

Well—does the cross bother you?

JEAN LEROUX

Oh! My Emperor—I would give my life—

EMPEROR

Then keep it, my friend.

OLD WOMAN

(presenting a glass on a server)

Here, my Emperor!

EMPEROR

(drinking then returning the cup to her)

Thanks, granny.

OLD WOMAN

No one will ever drink from that glass again, my Emperor. It will remain in the family until the hundredth generation.

EMPEROR

Good folks—let's go!

AIDE DE CAMP

(arriving at a gallop)

Sire! Sire!

EMPEROR

What's wrong?

AIDE DE CAMP

A column of troops coming from Vizille bars the highway and opposes our passage.

EMPEROR

What regiments involved?

AIDE DE CAMP

The 5th of the Line.

EMPEROR

The 5th of the Line. It's an old friend from Italy. Go see it, Cambronne, and tell them it's me.

CAMBRONNE

Sire, I won't have to—for they are here.

EMPEROR

And at charge step, even.

ALL

To arms, to arms.

EMPEROR

Hold your ranks! That's good. Disarm muskets and reverse cannons.

OFFICER

Sire, sire!

EMPEROR

Leave it to me, gentlemen, this is my concern! Soldiers!

COMMANDANT OF THE 5TH

Soldiers, don't listen to that man—he's bringing us civil war— soldiers, fire! Fire!

(The Emperor goes toward the soldiers.)

EMPEROR

(opening his uniform)

Soldiers of the 5th of the Line—if there is one among you who wishes to kill his general, his Emperor, he can—here I am!

ALL THE SOLDIERS

(throwing down their muskets)

Long Live the Emperor! Long Live the Emperor!

EMPEROR

Come on boys, come on! Ah, you are worthy, noble Frenchmen.

Come on, come on. Some tricolor cockades for these brave men.

SOLDIERS

(opening a band box)

Hey. We've got plenty, Sire.

EMPEROR

Come—that's good. Soldiers of the 5th of the Line I am satisfied with you. You too, you are my children.

(giving them a tricolor flag)

AN OLD SOLDIER

(pulling an Eagle from his knapsack)

Here's the cuckoo. Well, if you're satisfied with us, if we are your children—make us your avant garde!

EMPEROR

Agreed.

ALL

Bravo! Brave! Long Live the Emperor!

EMPEROR

Forward march, my friend, forward march. Bye granny.

OLD WOMAN

Goodbye, my Emperor.

(to peasants)

Well, aren't you folks going to say goodbye?

BASTIEN

(to peasants)

No need—we're going with him.

(The drums roll—they all march off, except the old woman.)

BLACKOUT

ACT V
SCENE 13

Colonel Bertrand's room.

BERTRAND

It's no use arguing, my dear France, something strange happened here the other night. I heard some noise, some threats, something like the clank of weapons—why did you leave me so hurriedly? What happened that my old friend, General Michel, and Colonel Gerard my companion in arms were here, in my house without my being told?

FRANCE

But, father, Victor told you—they were only passing by, they were going to embark at Toulon to join the army of Italy where Victor expects to join them one day or another.

BERTRAND

Why—Victor—himself—where is he? why is it since that night I haven't seen him?

FRANCE

Father, I told you—he went himself to Paris to solicit from the ministers of war his part in that activity.

BERTRAND

Listen, France—you are deceiving me here—

FRANCE

Father!

BERTRAND

For the last week you've been suffering and frightened.

FRANCE

Me?

BERTRAND

You—your voice is no longer the same—you hand is cold and trembling, you shiver suddenly as if you expected bad news from one minute to the next. Look France, tell me everything. I can tell from the way you're breathing, you are ready to cry.

FRANCE

Father!

(aside)

My God! My God! What to say? What to do?

FORTUNIO

(entering)

Pardon, excuse me if I disturb you, Colonel, but it's is Mr. Victor.

BERTRAND and FRANCE

Victor?

FORTUNIO

Yes, he's come from Paris—he's obtained what he desired and he wants to say goodbye to you—before—before he leaves.

BERTRAND

Where is he?

FORTUNIO

He's climbing the stairs. Come, come, Mr. Victor, the Colonel is waiting for you.

FRANCE

(low)

Fortunio.

FORTUNIO

(low)

Condemned, Miss, condemned! Only he has permission—oh, wait, I'm choking.

BERTRAND

(waiting at the door, arms extended)

Victor, Victor, where are you?

(Victor enters, escorted by a dozen soldiers who wait in the antechamber. The door remains open through the scene.)

VICTOR

(after signaling the soldier)

Here I am, father, here I am.

BERTRAND

Oh, how good it makes me feel to find you again, my poor Victor, to feel you near me, to press you in my arms.

VICTOR

Father.

FRANCE

(aside)

Oh! Oh! My God!

FORTUNIO

(aside)

Sonofabitch!

BERTRAND

You've no idea what strange thought I've had—it was a vague and somber uneasiness that nothing could combat. It was no use for your sister to tell me you were in Paris looking for a position. It seemed that an inner voice told me she was lying.

(to France)

Excuse me, France, I ought to know that angels never lie.

FRANCE

Father.

BERTRAND

And you were saying, Victor?

VICTOR

Well, father, I said that all my wishes are fulfilled, you must be astonished that at my age, having your glorious military career before me as an example—I remained with you, unemployed, useless—well, father, it won't be that way anymore. The Emperor calls me to him. The Grand Army is camped before Alexandria and I am going to join him there.

BERTRAND

Go, my child—it's a more beautiful country than Italy—at each step you reach over history, at each halt, you camp on a field of victory—and when do you leave?

VICTOR

I am ordered not to stop, father—just time enough to press you to my heart, time to say goodbye to you—that's all the time I have.

BERTRAND

Go, my friend, you have noble and beautiful examples there and will be near a master who knows how to reward. One day you'll wear on your chest a cross that reads—Honor and Country. Let those words be the guide to your thought and actions at all times. So, for being brave, I don't have to say anything on that account.

VICTOR

Thanks, father.

BERTRAND

Wait!

VICTOR

What, father?

BERTRAND

I want to give you a gift.

VICTOR

Your sword!

BERTRAND

You know this is a gift that the Emperor gave me at Moscow. My sword was shattered by a cannon and he gave me this.

VICTOR

Father, such a weapon is much too precious to leave the person to whom it was given. It's a family inheritance which must remain here, near you—on an altar—this weapon could be stolen from me or taken from me if I am made prisoner.

BERTRAND

It will remind you you mustn't surrender.

VICTOR

Well, I will kill myself, doubtless, but after my death it will belong to the first to come and tear it from my hands—no, father, no—keep this sword. Now, will you permit me to say goodbye to my sister?

BERTRAND

France, you hear?

FRANCE

(in Victor's arms)

Yes, father, yes.

VICTOR

(low to France)

Here, France, here are letters dated from different towns in Italy. You will read them successively to father so he will remain unaware as long as possible. Finally, a last will announce to him that I am wounded—mortally wounded. It must give him the supreme joy of believing his son died on the battlefield.

BERTRAND

Well, where are you then?

VICTOR

Here I am.

BERTRAND

What were you saying to France—? She's crying.

VICTOR

I was telling her what I am going to tell you, father—our wars are terrible wars—our battles, bloody battles, perhaps this is our last goodbye.

BERTRAND

What kind of ideas are these?

VICTOR

Yes, they are false, exaggerated, I know it, act as if they were true, father, embrace me as if we were never to see each other again—bless me as if I were about to die.

BERTRAND

These are somber omens, my child, and if they were coming on the even of a battle, they would frighten me—but with the aid of God, Victor, it won't be that way—on the contrary, I don't know why—I am full of hope and joy—I see you returning captain, colonel—what do I know? come, come, my child—come let me embrace you, come let me hug you.

VICTOR

Dear father.

BERTRAND

Well, what's wrong?

FORTUNIO

Colonel—look—you see—

VICTOR

Shut up, Fortunio.

FORTUNIO

Shut up, Fortunio, shut up—well, no, I don't wish to shut up—I am revolted.

FRANCE

What's he going to say?

FORTUNIO

I tell you, it will anger God to deceive his father this way and tell him 'au revoir' when he must say good bye forever.

VICTOR

Fortunio.

FORTUNIO

I tell you it's a sacrifice you are going to make. I tell you not to make it.

VICTOR

Father! Father! Don't believe him.

BERTRAND

(pulling away from Victor's hand)

Come, Fortunio, come—speak, my old friend—I know that you never think I am listening—what is it?

FORTUNIO

I say we are old soldiers, my colonel and that we know what unhappiness is.

BERTRAND

Yes, well—

FORTUNIO

I say that you are a father, I say that if I was one—it seems to me I would never pardon those who allowed me to leave my child without knowing where he is going—it seems to me I would curse those who made me believe my child was living when he was dead.

FRANCE and VICTOR

Ah! My God!

BERTRAND

Fortunio! Fortunio! What are you saying! Explain yourself.

FORTUNIO

Oh—the explanation is quite simple. The Emperor is no longer on the throne. The Emperor is a prisoner on the Isle of Elba—Mr. Victor conspired for the Emperor—he's condemned to death and he's come to say goodbye to you because they're going to shoot him. Indeed, the soldiers are here.

VICTOR and FRANCE

(bursting into tears)

Oh!

FORTUNIO

My word, too bad! The truth above all. That's my way of thinking.

BERTRAND

Fortunio, your hand. Thanks my friend. Oh, my children, it's very wicked to have deceived me like this.

VICTOR

Father, don't be angry with my sister. My sister is innocent. The idea was mine. I, suspecting your despair and knowing the story of that ring and the poison it contains, and knowing the oath you took to the Emperor—invented and maintained this long lie. It would be too cruel of you to reproach me for it now—now that I am going to die.

BERTRAND

Yes, and it's I who kill you—for, I remember I was the one who told the Prefect—Victor, my child, pardon your father—

(taking Victor in his arms)

Ah, my son! My Victor!

FORTUNIO

Colonel!

BERTRAND

Yes, you are right. We are men and not children or women. Tears and moans are for women—we have courage, we have strength. Come my child! It takes only an instant and it's over. It's a step to overcome. You will overcome it won't you, my son—head held high?

VICTOR

Oh—yes, father.

BERTRAND

Anyway—it's death, but a soldier's death! Suppose they told you: "Go die on the breach of a fort"—you would go, right?

VICTOR

Oh—yes, father.

PREFECT

You will go without flinching, without wincing, without weakening—and you would receive death head held high and with a proud eye?

VICTOR

I will receive it so, don't worry.

BERTRAND

Let's see.

(looking for Victor's heart)

VICTOR

There, father, you see—it beats as usual and if it pulses a bit more than usual, it does so, not from fear of death but from sadness at leaving you.

BERTRAND

Fine, my child, I am satisfied with you.

(low)

Anyway, don't worry, we won't be separated for long.

VICTOR

Father!

BERTRAND

Silence.

(turning to the solders)

Sergeant.

SERGEANT

Here I am, Colonel.

BERTRAND

You are an old soldier.

SERGEANT

I date from the Pyramids. We were together, my Colonel.

BERTRAND

My brave—your hand.

SERGEANT

Here it is, Colonel.

PREFECT

If he asks for no blindfold?

SERGEANT

No blindfold.

BERTRAND

If he asks to order the fire?

SERGEANT

He will order it.

BERTRAND

And you will tell your men to aim there?

(he points to the heart)

He's a child you see. He mustn't suffer.

SERGEANT

Don't worry.

FORTUNIO

By God—am I mistaken. It seems to me I have remorse.

BERTRAND

Victor.

VICTOR

Father.

BERTRAND

Have you taken leave of your sister?

VICTOR

Yes, father.

BERTRAND

Well, then.

VICTOR

Yes, they are waiting—and I mustn't keep them waiting. Goodbye, goodbye, dear father.

BERTRAND

(calling him)

Victor—once more the last—go—

(pushing him away)

Go, my son—go.

FRANCE

Ah—father, dear father!

(Victor leaves with the soldiers.)

BERTRAND

Well, what of it? He's a soldier who's going to die. That's all. And who is he going to die for—for the Emperor in other words. The benefactor of his family; for him I swore to die myself if he lost his throne—the father failed in his oath; the son fulfills it, that's well.

FRANCE

Father! Father!

BERTRAND

Well, yes, hug me, my daughter. Anyway, aren't you staying with me? Do you think all other fathers are happier than I? Oh, I have nothing to complain of, God be thanked. Victor could be an only child and then I would remain alone, but you are here, France. You will never leave me except to rejoin Emmanuel—for I understand—Emmanuel is at Elba, allied with the Emperor and I am the one that separates you. Two children who love each other, two hearts which beat as one. Damn, you must forgive me, my child—I didn't know.

FRANCE

Oh! Father! Father!

BERTRAND

No—I want to be alone a few moments, you understand—I need to compose myself, so long as I have you here, you see I think too much of your brother. Your voice reminds me of his. Leave me alone a moment, and you, too, Fortunio.

FORTUNIO

You are not angry with me, Colonel?

BERTRAND

No, oh, no! You felt it was a crime to deceive me.

FRANCE

A crime!

BERTRAND

Well—as it was not you who deceived me—as it was your brother—look, France, are you going to disobey me?

FRANCE

Oh!

BERTRAND

Listen, you will pray in the meantime—and in ten minutes you will send me Fortunio—go, go—take France—Fortunio.

FORTUNIO

Come, miss.

(Reaching the door—France stops.)

FRANCE

(low to Fortunio)

Wretch! Don't you see he wants to be alone to kill himself.

FORTUNIO

Oh! Then you are right, Miss. Don't leave him—don't leave him—goodbye, Colonel—we are going away—goodbye.

(Fortunio leaves, but France steps aside.)

BERTRAND

(motionless and holding his breath)

Ah! Here I am, alone at last! I promised Victor we would not be separated for long. I will fulfill two oaths by fulfilling that one.

FRANCE

(aside)

Oh—I knew it!

BERTRAND

There must be a pencil on this table.

(pulling the ring from his finger, he kisses it and places it near him)

Let's write.

(taking a pen, he writes awkwardly on a sheet of paper)

Dear France, goodbye, my darling child. Forgive your father for leaving you. But you have already prolonged my life with a pious lie.

(France quietly comes forward and takes the ring, replacing it with the medallion of her mother. The Colonel finishes and fumbles for the ring.)

BERTRAND

France's medallion. how could she have forgotten it? Its' a sign her mother is waiting for me. I'm coming, I'm coming.

(fumbling for the ring)

Where's the ring? Never mind—I have my pistols on the chimney.

(groping)

FRANCE

(aside)

Oh—my God!

(She substitutes a crucifix hanging at the head of the bed for the pistols.)

BERTRAND

(finding the crucifix)

This is witness that I have never doubted you.

(kissing the crucifix)

But where are my pistols?

(after fumbling without finding them)

Never mind. I still have my sword. Victor refused it. But it will serve me well.

(France rushes to get it but bumps into her father)

France.

FRANCE

Father, father—pity your daughter.

BERTRAND

Oh! Oh! My God! Have pity on me!

(tumult in the street)

Do you hear? Do you hear? They're going to shoot him. Oh Victor! Oh, my child—my child!

FORTUNIO

(outside)

Colonel! Colonel! Open! Open!

FRANCE

What's happening?

FORTUNIO

Joy! Miracle! Happiness! The Emperor's landed. The Emperor's at Vizille, the Emperor.

BERTRAND

The Emperor's landed, you say? You are mad?

FORTUNIO

Listen.

VOICES

(in the street)

The Emperor! The Emperor! Long Live the Emperor!

BERTRAND

My God! My God! If he's come in time! Bring me to him!

FRANCE

My brother! My brother!

(to Fortunio)

Ah, you said it—joy and miracle.

FRANCE

Come, father, come!

BERTRAND

The Emperor! The Emperor! Ah—come, France, come Fortunio!

(they leave entwined.)

BLACKOUT

ACT V
SCENE 14

The Port of Vizille at Grenoble. The city is lit up in the distance.

An officer, commanding fire on Lamure. Soldiers silent under arms. The people are noisy.

THE PEOPLE

The Emperor! The Emperor! The Emperor's coming. The Emperor is arriving.

A MAN

They sent the 5th of the Line against him and it went over to him.

OFFICER

Well, yes, he's the Emperor, but don't worry, he won't enter Grenoble like Vizille—Grenoble is a fortified city—Grenoble has fine walls—solid gates, a loyal garrison.

THE PEOPLE

The Emperor! Open the gates to the Emperor. The keys to the gates. The keys—the keys!

OFFICER

The keys to the gates? Here—

(throwing them into a well)

Go find them where they are now.

(noises, murmurs)

Soldiers, do your duty.

(The soldiers push back the people.)

(The Sergeant comes in with Victor and the escort of soldiers.)

SERGEANT

Pardon, pardon, comrades. This is duty—a sad duty. Let us pass.

(he passes with the escort and goes to the officer)

Officer!

OFFICER

What is the matter?

SERGEANT

This young man who conspired for the Emperor—you know, the son of Colonel Bertrand—must he still be executed?

OFFICER

He is condemned?

SERGEANT

Yes.

OFFICER

Has the hour of execution come?

SERGEANT

Yes.

OFFICER

Have you received a counter-order?

SERGEANT

No.

OFFICER

Well, let justice be done.

SERGEANT

It's that—as the—other is coming and will probably be here by evening.

OFFICER

All the more reason, sir—a great example will have been given.

SERGEANT

Then open the gates.

OFFICER

The gates are closed—and I am here to prevent their being opened.

SERGEANT

I cannot shoot him here.

OFFICER

You have the town graveyard. Open the Postern gate.

SERGEANT

That's the order?

OFFICER

That's the order. Go.

SERGEANT

Come, Mr. Victor, you must follow me.

VICTOR

Why it seems to me I cannot refuse.

SERGEANT

(descending through the postern gate)

This way, come.

(Uproar among the people.)

VICTOR

My friends, I don't regret my life, since I am dying for the Emperor. Long live the Emperor!

(They disappear. The uproar among the people redoubles.)

MAN OF THE PEOPLE

Are they going to shoot this poor young man, all the same? Even though the Emperor is coming?

A VOICE

Do you hear the drum? Do you hear?

(The drum can be heard in the distance.)

BERTRAND

(enters escorted by France and Fortunio)

My friends, my friends—you haven't seen him?

MAN OF THE PEOPLE

Ah! It's Colonel Bertrand—it's the father. Poor father!

BERTRAND

My son, Victor! They said they took him this way. You will save him won't you, my friends? You won't let them shoot him? He conspired for the Emperor. But is that a crime? If I hadn't been blind, I would have conspired with him. Let them shoot me with him! Let them shoot me.

FRANCE

Father!

BERTRAND

Fortunio—where is he? Ask, where he is—find out—you who are not blind!

MAN OF THE PEOPLE

(to Fortunio)

Here, here—that way—they took him that way—through the postern gate.

(Fortunio goes down through the postern. An explosion is heard—he reappears pale and staggering.)

BERTRAND

Victor! Victor!

(he falls on his knees)

FRANCE

Father! Father! Help—help!

(Victor rushes from the postern without his shirt and his vest.)

VICTOR

Long Live the Emperor!

FRANCE

My brother!

BERTRAND

Victor! Victor, living! Impossible. It's really him. Let me touch you. But that report?

VICTOR

These brave folks, seeing the Emperor arrive, fired in the air instead of firing at me.

BERTRAND

Ah! My God! My God! What grace! What a miracle! What joy!

VICTOR

(placing the hand of the Sergeant in his father's hand)

Our Savior, father, our savior.

FORTUNIO

(at the postern)

This way, Sappers—this way. Break open the gates.

(The Sappers of the 5th break down the gate. The Emperor appears.)

ALL

Long Live the Emperor!

EMPEROR

Thanks, kids, thanks.

BERTRAND

The Emperor's voice.

VICTOR and FRANCE

Yes father—it's him, him!

EMPEROR

(entering on horseback)

Frenchmen, it's for you alone, and the brave men of the army, that I still glorify myself with my crown and my power.

ALL

Long Live the Emperor!

BERTRAND

(on his knees)

Sire! Sire!

EMPEROR

(getting off his horse)

Ah! It's you, my old friend, Bertrand. In my arms, in my arms!

BERTRAND

My son! My Emperor! Ah, I can die now.

THE MAYOR

(at the head of the town council)

Sire, Your Majesty's lodging his been prepared at the town hall.

EMPEROR

Thanks, gentlemen, I'll stay with my friend, Colonel Bertrand. We have a marriage to celebrate right, Emmanuel?

EMMANUEL and FRANCE

Sire!

EMPEROR

Soldiers. Tomorrow at dawn we march on Paris!

(Acclamations, trumpets, shouts of "Long Live the Emperor!")

CURTAIN

POSTSCRIPT

Some critics have judged *The Barricade at Clichy* without having seen it, or having seen it without hearing it; pretending that the play is written "from the point of view of the Élysée Palace."

I deny having ever created a political play from any other point of view than republicanism.

Richard Darlington, *The Girondins*, *Catalina*, those are for the past.

The Barricade at Clichy, that's for the present.

If Bonaparte had had in his heart the thoughts I put in his mouth, God would have made him through his victories, the active agent of our liberty, instead of making him, through his fall, the passive instrument of our emancipation. Now perhaps it will be asked, why did I put in the mouth of Napoleon thoughts of liberty that he never had in his heart?

To this I will reply that the theatre is not a course in history but a tribune through which the poet expands and propagates his own ideas. That my ideas, ideas that I think good according to democratic equality as I understand it, acquire a new power in the mouth of a man whom the people have made into a demi-god and that, on the whole, since they have put Napoleon on a pedestal, it's better that the people believe he is the agent of European liberty rather than the representative of despotism in France.

Someday I promise myself to write a history of Napoleon and I hope it will be one of the first to measure this giant with a philosophic glance to whom God gave feet of clay and a head of bronze.

—Alex. Dumas

ABOUT THE AUTHOR

Frank J. Morlock has written and translated many plays since retiring from the legal profession in 1992. His translations have also appeared on Project Gutenberg, the Alexandre Dumas Père web page, Literature in the Age of Napoléon, Infinite Artistries. com, and Munsey's (formerly Blackmask). In 2006 he received an award from the North American Jules Verne Society for his translations of Verne's plays. He lives and works in México.

www.ingramcontent.com/pod-product-compliance
Lightning Source LLC
Chambersburg PA
CBHW030916090426
42737CB00007B/212